MISSISSIPPI "A" SISTER'S JUSTICE

Hidden Family Secrets

JEROME GENTRY

"For nothing is hidden that will not become evident, nor anything secret that will not be known and come to light"

(NASB- Luke 8:17)

Copyright © 2024
JEROME GENTRY

All rights are reserved. No part of this book may be reproduced, distributed, or transmitted in any form or by any means, including photocopying, recording, or other electronic or mechanical methods, without the prior written permission of the author, except in the case of brief quotations embodied in critical reviews and certain other noncommercial uses permitted by copyright law. For permission requests, write to the author at the address provided in the acknowledgments section of this book.

Printed in the United States of America

First Printing Edition, 2024

Library of Congress Control Number: 2024917817

ISBN: 978-0-9819027-6-0

For Additional Information about this story, E-mail: jeromegentry@aol.com

Dedication

This book is dedicated to my three loving and supportive daughters: Deanna Lashay Gentry, born September 1991. Mia Nicole Gentry, who was born in May 2001, and Ma Leanna Bejec Gentry, who was born in March 2021. It is also dedicated to the many individuals who have suffered in their lives from the lack of support throughout the traumatic experiences that they have experienced in their lives.

Contents

Dedication IV
Author's Note VI
Preface IX
Introduction XIV
Chapter One: The Unforeseen Decision 1
Chapter Two: Open Plea's Uncertain Fate 11
Chapter Three: Unveiling The Past Trauma 21
Chapter Four: The Protective Sister's Dilemma 39
Chapter Five: Confronting The Legal System 52
Chapter Six: Statute Of Limitations - Child Molestation 64
Chapter Seven: The Journey Of Healing 81
Ways To Heal Your Childhood Trauma 92
Ways To Support A Loved One Who Experienced Childhood Abuse 94
Chapter Eight: Understanding Child Molestation 98
Coping With The Shock Of Intrafamilial Sexual Abuse 101
Child Sexual Abuse 105
Why Adults Fail To Protect Children 107
References 114

Author's Note

Jerome Gentry, a Certified Financial Services Auditor, not only has an impressive professional background but has also left his mark as an author and filmmaker. His literary works include "Mississippi's Uncovered Glory" (2008) and "The Ultimate Business Bible" (2009), capturing his insights and expertise in the financial realm. Moreover, he ventured into the world of documentary production with "Beyond The Glory" in 2016, showcasing his multifaceted talents.

The most remarkable aspect of Jerome's life, however, is his unwavering commitment to his three daughters, who share an unbreakable bond despite being from three separate marriages. Deanna Lashay Gentry, born in 1991, is Jerome's firstborn from his initial marriage, which lasted from 1986 to 1998. Subsequently, his marriage in 2000 brought forth his second daughter, Mia Nicole Gentry, in 2001, before ending in 2004.

Through the trials and triumphs of life, Jerome embraced love once more in 2020 through marriage amidst the challenges of a global pandemic. This union bore his third daughter, Maria-Leanna Bejec Gentry, in 2021. What's particularly captivating is the thought behind Maria-Leanna's name, which pays homage to both her elder sisters. A fusion of "Deanna" and "Mia," her name symbolizes the enduring connection between the three sisters, transcending mere family ties.

Jerome's academic journey led him to graduate with a Bachelor of Science in accounting, followed by a distinguished Master of Business Administration (MBA) degree. His professional credentials extend beyond academia, as he holds licenses as an insurance and real estate broker alongside his Certified Financial Services Auditor (CFSA) designation. Although retired, Jerome remains active in real estate, retaining his broker's license.

His career spans the banking industry, state government, and the nonprofit sector, with entrepreneurial ventures in the tax industry and franchise ownership in business coaching. Notably, his expertise garnered him a platform on CNN's "Talk Back Live" and earned him features in various publications and interviews across different media outlets. Amidst these diverse experiences, Jerome discovered a deep-seated passion for writing, driven by the need to commemorate his brother's untimely passing, culminating in the publication "Mississippi's Uncovered Glory" in 2008.

Figure 1: Jerome with his three daughters spending family-time together: Deanna LaShay, Mia Nicole and Maria-Leanna.

Preface

First and foremost, I want to express my profound pride in my daughter, Deanna. Her academic journey from Madison Central High School in Madison, MS, to earning a degree in economics from The University of Mississippi (Ole Miss), followed by the pursuit of obtaining a Master's Degree in Computer Science, is a testament to her dedication and determination. Her brief stint as an intern in Washington, DC, where she worked for a US Congressman, further showcases her ambition and commitment to making a difference.

One poignant moment that truly reflects Deanna's character is when she took the initiative to inform then-Governor Haley Barbour of Mississippi about her great-grandmother's 105th birthday. This act of respect and acknowledgment led to Governor Barbour signing a proclamation designating October 31, 2004, as her great-grandmother's Day in Mississippi, underscoring Deanna's reverence for family and tradition.

On a personal note, Deanna's presence has had a profound impact on my life. In his book "Mississippi's Uncovered Glory," he wrote about the joy and fulfillment her birth brought him. Her resilience and strength have breathed new life into him, rekindling his zest for life and purpose.

Despite facing her own internal struggles, often without the support she needs, Deanna continues to uplift others and make a positive impact in the world. Her unwavering determination and compassion serve as a source of inspiration for us all.

Life's purpose can be enigmatic, but Deanna's purpose is unmistakable: to enhance the lives of those around her. While destiny may unfold according to a higher plan, our choices and actions shape our journey. Through the highs and lows, Deanna's resilience and unwavering spirit shine bright, illuminating the path forward for us all.

*Figure 2: Deanna standing with U.S. Congressman:
The Honorable Gregg Harper.*

Figure 3: Deanna attending a conference in Washington D.C. while in conversation with U.S. Congressman: The Honorable John Lewis.

Figure 4: Deanna in 2004 with me and then Mississippi's Governor; The Honorable Haley Barbour. This was the meeting when Deanna talked to Governor Barbour about honoring her Great-Grandmother.

Introduction

This book is a personal account that tells the story of my precious daughter's journey. I have three daughters: Deanna Lashay, Mia Nicole, and Maria-Leanna. This story is mainly about Deanna. However, Mia plays one of the most important roles in the story.

Deanna made a terrible life-changing decision that I believe could have been avoided from both; a law enforcement and personal standpoint. The effects of this decision brought back some dark, forgotten, and hidden childhood traumas that had been buried. Furthermore, the local news media outlets reported that the decision was incorrect. Unfortunately, in many instances, news outlets do not report the correct news, and society often just accepts what is reported. This was the case with the story about Deanna.

I also delved deeply into the legal aspects that Deanna faced as our family dealt with all the emotions surrounding her uncharacteristic decision. I have always been a champion for my girls and will continue to be as long as I live. Deanna's life is more than just about that one dreadful day, and I want those who read this book to know who she is as a person. Therefore, I am writing this book to provide accurate information about the events leading up to that dreadful day and the aftermath of dealing with the legal system. There is accountability for all situations that occur, and this book will help in understanding that process of accountability.

This book also discusses how families deal with childhood trauma and the effects it has on individuals as adults if it goes untreated. In many cases, we let the victim down by not helping them deal with their issues. Often, the perpetrator receives more sympathy than the victim when the victim is not believed. It can be an even more serious situation when close family members of the victim are in denial that anything even happened.

Research has repeatedly shown that child sexual abuse can have a very serious impact on physical and mental health. Depending on the severity and number of traumas experienced, child sexual abuse can have wide-reaching and long-lasting effects. Those who have suffered multiple traumas and received little parental support may develop post-traumatic stress disorder, depression, and anxiety. The adults and the systems that were in place to protect Deanna did not do so. For me, the thoughts of that time bring back emotional memories that were buried. I felt, many years ago, that I was the ONLY ONE fighting for her. Now, after this situation so many years later, I feel as though I lost that fight. However, the battle is not over, and the fight continues for her.

Figure 5: Deanna with her sister Mia Nicole attending her graduation ceremony at The University of Mississippi (Ole Miss) in 2014. Deanna graduated with her Bachelor of Science degree in economics and a minor in Biology.

CHAPTER ONE
The Unforeseen Decision

Life is a terrifying mix of capriciousness and injustice in equal measures. One day, you're enduring the monotony of your mundane routine. The next, you struggle to persevere through a storm. Unfortunate times don't come with a disclaimer. When your world turns upside down, it often feels like a punch in the gut. You don't see it coming, and it leaves you breathless, battered, and bruised. Against the pull of circumstances, you feel helpless, desperate to make it out of that hell. Most often, it's the unpredictability of life that feels so jarring. The unforeseen events leave us scrambling for any semblance of rhyme and reason.

I recall the moment clear as day when life was thrown into disarray. It was August 12, 2021, a day that forever altered the course of my life. The clock struck 6:00 in the evening when my phone began to ring. As I got the buzzing phone out of my pocket, the screen displayed an unfamiliar number. Curiosity gripped me, and I answered the call, unaware of the storm that awaited me on the other end.

To my surprise, it was my beloved daughter, Deanna. "Daddy," she spoke in a voice laced with fear and desperation, "I have been arrested for attempted murder."

My heart skipped a beat. However, my mind was unable to process the gravity of her words. My subsequent thought was: *This is some practical prank, a twisted joke played at my expense.*

As our conversation unfolded, reality crashed into me like a tidal wave. Deanna's words pierced through the fog of disbelief, leaving me no choice but to face the harsh truth. However, the reality was jarring. Throughout her life, I had never known Deanna to be involved in any domestic altercations, nor had she ever faced the daunting prospect of being arrested or confined behind prison walls. The whole ordeal left me utterly bewildered, struggling to make sense of this sudden change in her behavior. My mind raced, desperately trying to grasp the reality of the situation, but the pieces refused to fit together.

After a few minutes, I found my voice, "How did this happen, Deanna?"

"Talk to Mia. She'll explain everything." Little did I know that talking to Mia would lead me to another trail of shocking revelations. My beloved daughter, Deanna, continued, "Daddy, I was not trying to shoot anybody."

At her words, I felt a wave of reassurance pass over me. Yet, I still couldn't bring myself to believe it. I knew that Deanna possessed a gun. She had revealed it to me a few months prior, and it had been properly registered. We also even had target practice on several occasions. Given that my two daughters resided together in our older neighborhood, having some form of protection within the confines of their home didn't seem like a bad idea. However, it had never crossed my mind that I would have to explicitly caution her not to go somewhere and start shooting at just anyone. The notion of her venturing out and firing shots at another individual was beyond the realm of possibilities for me.

After what felt like an eternity, she spoke again in a defeated voice, "I was just calling to let you know. Can you help me get out of here?"

"Where are you?" I asked.

"At the Rankin County Sheriff's Department," she answered.

Surprised, I repeated, "You are at the Rankin County Sheriff's Department?"

"Yes," she answered.

"Okay, Deanna," I replied. I knew I had to do whatever it took to help her. "Has a bond been set? Can I come and get you?"

She turned to someone in the room with her, and I strained to overhear their conversation. My heart raced with anticipation, waiting for her response. Finally, she relayed their words back to me, her voice laced with disappointment. "No bond has been set yet, and they said it's unlikely to happen until the beginning of next week."

"Okay," I replied, trying to steady my voice, "I'll start contacting an attorney, Deanna. We'll find a way to navigate through this nightmare."

With a heavy sigh, we reluctantly ended the telephone conversation. My mind buzzed with several questions. Why was my daughter trying to shoot someone? Why was she at the Rankin County Sheriff's Department? At the time, I had no idea that the incident took place in

Pearl. Later, I found out that the Rankin County courthouse is the jurisdiction where a person would be held and tried for incidents happening in Pearl, Mississippi. Later, I also learned the cause behind my daughter's actions. However, at the time, I couldn't make sense of anything. It was late evening, and I knew I couldn't contact an attorney at that time. So, I decided to wait until the next morning to seek legal counsel. However, there was one person I needed to talk to immediately - Mia. I needed her insight into Deanna's situation to understand the events that had led to this nightmare.

Without wasting a moment, I dialed Mia's number. As her voice filled the line, I could sense the worry and concern that mirrored my own. She began to recount the details, revealing a shocking truth that I had been oblivious to until now. The person Deanna was being charged with attempting to murder was Mia's ex-boyfriend, a man I had never even heard of before.

Mia explained that he had shown up at their home, igniting a physical altercation between him and Deanna. She recounted the chaos. Deanna and her ex-boyfriend had gotten into an altercation. It started with exchanging words and physical contact with Mia's ex-boyfriend, pushing Deanna down before fleeing the scene in his car. I later found out that Mia's ex-boyfriend was a lot bigger than Deanna. He stood about six feet, six inches, with a medium build. Mia emphasized that he was never supposed to be near their house again, as Deanna had previously called the Jackson Police Department when he had shown up, but the police had failed to do their job the first time, leaving the girls feeling helpless and desperate. The only thing they did was advise him not to come back to that address again. Mia had always been timid, so she could easily be oppressed into silence. However, Deanna was not one to be intimated with, so she took matters into her own hands. In a fit of fury, Deanna retrieved a gun from the house and followed after him. Her actions were dictated by her desire to protect her sister, but unfortunately, they got her into trouble instead. All the revelation left me speechless.

As the pieces of the puzzle started to come together, Mia disclosed another unsettling fact. Her ex-boyfriend had assaulted her just a few weeks before this incident, on July 24th, 2021. Mia and Deanna had gone to the Pearl Police Department to file a report, hoping for justice to be served. However, Mia expressed her disappointment, stating that the Pearl Police Department seemed unhelpful and gave them the impression that filing a formal assault charge would yield no results. A facts and circumstances sheet was written up by the Pearl Police Department, and a case number was assigned, but no formal charges were filed.

The weight of the situation bore down on me. I had no inkling of the events that had unfolded prior to this situation concerning Deanna, as they had kept me in the dark, striving for independence. It saddened me to realize that they had been shouldering this earth-shattering burden all alone, trying to handle it themselves. So much had been going on in my daughters' lives, and I was oblivious to everything. If only the police departments had done their duties, if only they had provided the guidance and supported these young women desperately needed. Deanna wouldn't be caught in this dire situation, and Mia's ex-boyfriend would have faced the consequences of his actions.

After talking to Mia, I grew increasingly restless. The nightmare had just begun. The next day, I decided to call Deanna's mom. I don't recall the exact details of my conversation with her. The only thing that stands out in my memory is her expressing concern about how this situation would be perceived in her community. At the time, I was taken aback by her comment and didn't have a response. Amidst those troubling circumstances, the thought hadn't even occurred to me. I was not concerned about what thoughts the community thought about Deanna's mom. I was only concerned about assisting Deanna in her time of despair. The consequences of this ordeal undoubtedly had far-reaching implications, and it became evident very soon.

The very next morning, I was jolted out of my restless sleep by the sound of my phone ringing. As I picked it up, my ears were met by the voice of a relative, their voice filled with concern and curiosity. They wanted to know about Deanna's situation, but I couldn't help but wonder how the news had spread so quickly. I asked them where they had heard about it, and they informed me that it was all over the news - Deanna shooting at her boyfriend.

"What?" I couldn't believe my ears.

With a sense of urgency, I corrected them, explaining that it wasn't Deanna's boyfriend but Mia's ex-boyfriend who was shot at. I added that the guy had been abusive towards Mia in the past, and Deanna wasn't trying to shoot him; in fact, she was forced by the circumstances. I assured my relative that we were going to be alright.

However, as I hung up the phone, a sense of unease settled within me. I felt compelled to investigate what was being reported about Deanna to understand the narrative that was being woven by the media.

As I delved into the local news outlets, shock coursed through me. The distorted and incorrect information being reported about Deanna was staggering. The headlines screamed sensationalized falsehoods, twisting the truth to grab attention. My anxiety heightened with every word I read.

"A woman arrested in Pearl for the attempted murder of her boyfriend."

According to Greg Flynn with the City of Pearl, "police arrested Deanna Gentry. She has been charged with shooting into an occupied dwelling and attempted murder."

These statements did not hold the complete truth. It was clear to me that the news outlets were more concerned about being the first to report any information rather than ensuring the accuracy of their reports. The comments made on the public forum regarding her were even more hurtful, consisting of disrespectful and derogatory remarks about her appearance. Some of the comments I read are written below:

- "Pearl Police rated her appearance a 10?"
- "5'-3" and 285......I like her at the nose guard."
- "What a dumbass. 29 years old and can't understand shooting at someone is a bad idea (and illegal). Central MS Corrections Facility is in Deanna's future. Hopefully, for about 25 years."
- "Bet she drops a few pounds in the slammer."
- "She should be damned glad to have any man, not shooting at the one who gave her the time of day. 285 pounds! Sheesh!"

The hurtful comments made by these individuals have the potential to exacerbate someone's depression, leading them to question their own self-worth and confidence. Even for those who didn't have existing mental health issues, reading such derogatory remarks about themselves could contribute to the development of deep-seated mental health problems. It is important to consider that the individuals making these statements were unaware of Deanna's personal struggles and the true circumstances surrounding the situation. They were unkindly commenting on someone that they had no genuine knowledge of and basing their judgments solely on what was reported by the local news outlet. It was incredibly painful to read such harsh words targeted at my daughter, and I was determined to get her out of this ordeal as soon as possible.

The day after Deanna's arrest was a blur of frantic activity. The following day, I reached out to the attorney and provided him with the limited information I had. I paid the attorney's retainer fee, and fortunately, he agreed to take on the case. I wanted Deanna's mom to be involved with Deanna's situation, so sometime later, I requested that she contribute a portion of the retainer fee, which she did. I have known this attorney for a significant amount of time, and he has always been highly regarded as a skilled and experienced legal professional.

Armed with the lawyer's advice, I took Mia to the Jackson police station, determined to file a restraining order against her ex-boyfriend. We were able to obtain a temporary 10-day restraining order, which provided a sense of relief. A few days later, I accompanied Mia to the Pearl Police Department to formally press assault charges against her ex-boyfriend.

As we began the process of filing the charges, I noticed Mia's demeanor change. She started to cry, and it was evident that something was troubling her deeply.

Concerned, I gently asked her, "Do you want to file these charges?" I was taken aback when she replied with a resounding "no." It was a shocking response, and I couldn't comprehend her reasoning at that moment.

Trying to understand her perspective, I mustered the courage to ask her another question, "Have you seen or talked with this ex-boyfriend since the incident with Deanna?"

My heart sank when she quietly answered, "Yes."

It was a revelation that left me speechless. I couldn't fathom how Mia could continue to have contact with someone who had caused so much harm.

"Your sister is in jail," I couldn't help but express my frustration. "She tried to protect you, and you're still... still talking to him?"

In a hushed voice, she admitted, "I know." It was a confession that carried the weight of guilt and the complexity of emotions, so I didn't probe further.

At that moment, it became clear to me that Mia was completely unaware of the gravity of the situation her sister was facing. It struck me how some individuals who are being abused have no realization of the abuse they are enduring. They may unknowingly return to the same toxic environment, unable to recognize the harm inflicted upon them.

When someone is being abused, it can feel like they're losing touch with themselves. The abuser often isolates the victim, creating a sense of dependency that can be really hard to break free from. It's almost like the victim feels the need to protect the person who's hurting them, even when they're the one who's suffering. It's like they're walking on eggshells, constantly trying to avoid setting off the abuser and hoping to keep the peace despite the harm they're enduring. In hindsight, I understand that Mia must have been experiencing those complex emotions. Although, I didn't know at the time when I took Mia to the Pearl Police Department, I later discovered disturbing details about her ex-boyfriend. He had a history of physically assaulting her, knocking her down, and even providing her with dangerous substances like hard alcohol.

When the guy faced no repercussions, Deanna believed that the system had failed Mia in providing the necessary protection, leaving her unsure of what steps to take. Witnessing Mia's ex-boyfriend back at their home on that day must have been a shocking sight for Deanna, fueling her anger and frustration. It was evident that Deanna's actions were driven by her deep concern for Mia's well-being. She yearned to shield her sister from harm. Unfortunately, her act of courage came with a price.

CHAPTER TWO
Open Plea's Uncertain Fate

Following the dreadful news, my life became a whirlwind of unaddressed tension and unspoken grief. Every night, I tossed and turned in bed, awaiting the fate that should happen to my daughter. Finally, I got a call from Deanna's lawyer. However, the news hit me like a ton of bricks. Two charges - attempted murder and shooting into a dwelling. The court set her bond at $250,000 per charge, a total of half a million dollars. It was like a punch to the gut. The first thing that crossed my mind was that the maximum sentence in this type of case is 40 years in prison. To my dismay, I later found out that it was more.

Deanna's lawyer's next words sent a fresh wave of despair through me. He explained that without a solid defense, things were looking grim. The presence of someone else in the house, Mia's ex-boyfriend's grandmother, shattered our hope of using self-defense. My mind raced back to the events leading up to this nightmare. The altercation with

Mia's ex had been a terrifying experience for her, but a horrible truth gnawed at me. While driving to his house, Deanna had an opportunity to turn back. A chance to walk away, to de-escalate the situation, and avoid this tragedy. But she didn't and I could understand why. However, due to her choice, any hope we might have clung to for a self-defense plea was gone.

When the lawyer quoted the bond amount of $500,000 cash, I found myself flabbergasted. It felt unreal and excessive. My mind raced, fueled by disbelief and a growing sense of panic. I knew of people charged with murder who faced lower bonds. The situation seemed unfair, and I started feeling spasms of anger at the system again.

The attorney tried to reassure me, explaining that he would request a hearing to try to get the bond reduced. However, the waiting period felt unendurable! Each second seemed to stretch into an eternity, becoming a reminder of the immense financial hurdle ahead.

As news of Deanna's situation spread, I received calls and texts from seemingly concerned family members. Their words of support started to grate on me after repeated inquiries about how they could help. When I finally shared the bond amount, I often got silence in return.

I realized that many of their offers of help were empty. My frustration grew. It seemed they were more interested in the details of Deanna's case than genuinely figuring out how to help. It made me bitter as I felt utterly alone in this crisis.

My takeaway from the experience was this: When someone is going through a tragedy, avoid asking, "what can I do to help?" unless you have a specific, actionable offer. Simply letting that person know you are thinking of them carries more weight than empty promises.

'$500,000 bond, attempted murder, shooting into a dwelling,' these words were a constant reminder of the nightmare unfolding before me. A few days later, a glimmer of hope emerged when Deanna's lawyer called with news of the bond hearing. He had argued that her lack of prior criminal history and no flight risk should factor in, and the judge agreed to a reduction. Relief washed over me, but it was tempered by the harsh reality that the bond was still a staggering $250,000, all in cash.

The lawyer introduced me to the concept of a bail bondman, someone who could guarantee the full amount for a smaller fee. He explained that the bail bondman would save me from having to come up with the entire sum myself. It sounded too good to be true. This "smaller fee" amounted to $30,000, which was a huge amount in my view. It was a non-refundable sum, and that felt like throwing money away. To lose $30,000 with no guarantee Deanna would stay out of trouble was a bitter pill to swallow.

Even with the lawyer's successful reduction of the bond to $250,000, a heavy burden fell on my shoulders.

I grappled with the decision. The thought of being out $250,000 in cash was daunting, but the idea of losing $30,000 with no guarantee was equally unsettling. Seeing my struggle, Deanna's lawyer offered another option - I could post the bond myself. He patiently explained the process, and after careful consideration, I decided to give it a try.

It wasn't easy, but with the lawyer's guidance, I navigated the cumbersome legal procedures, posted the cash, and finally secured Deanna's release on August 23rd, 2021.

Relief surged through me as Deanna walked out of the jail. But it was a bittersweet moment. The judge had ordered an ankle monitor, essentially placing Deanna under house arrest. Disappointment gnawed at me, but it was a small price to pay for her freedom, however limited.

Therefore, we started the long drive home, but it was charged with a tense silence. I finally broke it, asking Deanna what had happened. Her voice, shaky and laced with guilt, filled the car. "He came to the house," she began, referring to Mia's ex-boyfriend. "We argued, and I shouldn't have, but I just..."

She continued in a lower voice, "I went inside for my gun, and Mia tried to stop me. She told me to calm down, but all I could think about was how he'd hurt her before and how he'd hurt me. When I came back out, he was gone."

Deanna took a shuddering breath. "I got in the car, driven by anger. I saw him outside his house in the yard, and in a moment of madness, I pointed the gun at him. I swear, Dad, I was not trying to shoot him. I did point the gun at him, but at the last moment, I pointed the gun in another direction."

I heaved a sigh of relief. I really believe that Deanna was only trying to scare him because she felt utterly helpless and unsupported by anyone or anything during that period. She believed Mia had no protection against him. "Thank God you didn't," I choked out. "This could be so much worse."

In response, Deanna whispered, "I just wanted to protect Mia."

Deanna was emotionally fragile, grappling with the weight of her actions and the potential consequences. Therefore, I held back the urge to ask further questions, offering silent support.

A part of me knew this was just the beginning. Deep down, I harbored little hope that the charges would be dropped. However, I knew this wasn't a petty crime, not in the current climate of the country. In my heart, I knew Deanna's actions wouldn't be easily dismissed, especially considering the current state of gun violence throughout the country.

The wait was agonizing. For two years, we held our breath, hoping for any sign of reprieve. Then, on September 5th, 2023, the phone call we dreaded arrived. The Rankin County Sheriff's Department informed me that Deanna had been indicted and needed to appear at the Rankin County Sheriff's Department the next day.

My stomach lurched. I immediately called Deanna and her lawyer. The appointment time became etched in my mind: September 6th at 9:00 AM. We walked into the sheriff's department, bracing for the worse; Deanna was formally served with the indictment.

A sliver of hope peeked through the dense fog of despair as we scrutinized the indictment. One of the charges had been altered: "attempted murder" now read "attempted aggravated assault." Deanna and I clung to this seemingly minor detail. Attempted murder carried a life sentence, a terrifying prospect that had left us on edge. We assumed attempted aggravated assault meant 30 years; of course, it was a daunting sentence but infinitely better than life behind bars. We allowed ourselves a brief moment of relief.

Later, as I delved deeper into the legalese, a wave of terror washed over me. My initial relief was misplaced. A closer look revealed the harsh reality: attempted aggravated assault also carried a sentence of 20 years to life. My stomach churned. How could I have been so blind? Gratitude flooded me for not knowing this truth before Deanna's final sentencing. Ignorance, in this case, had been bliss.

In the original indictment, there were four offenses that the Grand Jurors had identified against Deanna, and the range of sentence was as follows:

Count I: Shooting into a Dwelling (1 year - 10 years), $5,000 fine

Count II: Drive-By Shooting (0 years - 30 years), $10,000 fine

Count III: Attempted Aggravated Assault (20 years - life)

Count IV: Shooting At or Into a Motor Vehicle (1 year - 5 years)

The gloomy reality was that each charge stemmed from the use of a firearm, making the uphill battle we faced even steeper.

Our circumstances looked bleak. The initial plea bargain from the Rankin County DA stated ten years for "shooting into a dwelling" and a staggering thirty years, with ten years suspended, for "drive-by shooting" - both served consecutively, adding up to a stolen thirty years of Deanna's life. In exchange, they were also willing to drop charges three and four if we agreed to this deal. Through the representation of Deanna's attorney, Deanna said that she would decline the plea deal. She expressed her intention to pursue a trial on all charges leveled against her, and I agreed with her decision.

The prosecutor came back to the table with a new offer. This time, it was 10 years for the first charge with 5 years suspended and 20 years for the second charge with 5 years suspended, again served consecutively. This meant a total of 20 years in prison. And just like before, they'd drop the remaining charges if we accepted this offer.

Deanna's face paled, mirroring the hollowness that threatened to consume me. A whirlwind of emotions swirled inside. How could this be happening? Deanna had been transformed from protector to potential prisoner, all because of someone who had already inflicted so much pain and havoc on my daughters' lives.

The lawyer explained the twisting legal system. "This judge," he stated, "won't entertain anything less than twenty years for a shooting case in Rankin County." The DA's offer, while seemingly concrete, was merely a suggestion. The judge could very well impose a harsher sentence, rendering our negotiations a cruel exercise in futility.

At his words, I felt a deep sense of despair settle upon me. Twenty years. The image of Deanna, my child, her youth and dreams bartered away in the sterile confines of a prison, was a vision so excruciating that it stole the very air from my lungs.

Naturally, we declined this offer as well and were looking to go to trial.

A day later, a glimmer of hope blossomed. The assistant DA offered an open plea on Counts 1 and 2. It wasn't a perfect solution, but it allowed Deanna to present her story and her character to the judge, a chance for him to see beyond the single, life-altering decision she made on August 12th, 2021.

In my opinion, I believe that the assistant district attorney thoroughly reviewed all the evidence in the case and demonstrated compassion toward Deanna. He believed that the offer and recommendations that he presented were the minimum that the judge would consider from him.

Deep down, I knew Deanna had no real defense in the traditional sense. Even if the young man had pushed her, even if he had hurt Mia before, the legal system saw things in stark black and white. She had time to "cool off" after he left the house, time to walk away from the situation, to report it to the authorities. In their eyes, she had crossed a line and taken matters into her own hands.

The open plea, with all its limitations, was the best option we had. It wasn't a question of guilt or innocence, of whether she fired the shots with someone inside the house. The reality was harsh – she was guilty, and the jury likely would have empathized with her motive, her desire to protect Mia. But empathy wouldn't erase the gravity of her actions; the four bullets that struck the house endangered the innocent grandmother inside.

We chose the open plea, although it was a difficult decision driven by the lack of better options. It was a gamble, a chance for Deanna's humanity, her remorse, to shine through, to sway the judge toward a more merciful sentence. What I considered one of the most dangerous aspects of taking the open plea option was that Deanna would give up her rights to appeal the decision of the judge. It would be a final sentence. As we navigated this uncharted territory, the feeling of dread lingered, but I held onto the hope that somehow, some way, we would get Deanna back home in a reasonable time that would be handed down by the court.

In the process of getting our presentations together for Deanna to present to the judge, Deanna mentioned to her attorney about being in counseling for the past two years since the incident. He saw an opportunity in this - perhaps her therapy records held insights and explanations for her actions on that fateful day. Time was ticking - the open plea hearing was set for November 20th, with the trial date following on December 5th, 2023.

The 20th of November arrived, and we entered the courtroom. Deanna entered her plea, her voice trembling slightly. But what happened next shattered the fragile hope we clung to. Instead of the expected wait for the trial, Deanna was immediately taken back into custody. The sentence, whatever it may be, would begin then and there.

Disappointment washed over me like a cold wave. We were robbed of the chance to say a proper goodbye, a loving farewell to my daughter. However, as I watched her wave from across the room, a small flicker of understanding ignited within me. Perhaps, in the face of the unexpected, this abrupt separation was the most merciful course of action. It spared us the agonizing wait. Amidst the sting of loss and the ache of uncertainty, I choose to believe it was for the best.

A few days after Deanna's unexpected detention, her lawyer called with news. He had received her counseling records, and his words held a hint of something unexpected - something he called "interesting." My heart pounded in my chest with a mixture of trepidation and a sliver of hope. Perhaps these records held the key to understanding Deanna's actions, a glimpse into the darkness that had shrouded her.

The report arrived on November 30th. As I devoured its contents, a wave of shock and profound sadness washed over me. It spoke of a young woman battling demons I never knew existed: depressive episodes, sudden behavioral changes, paranoia, and personality shifts. It mentioned poor hygiene and a chilling detail – a suicide attempt in her high school years. The report also revealed that she had been severely overweight.

These revelations were a gut punch. How could I have been so blind to her struggles? The weight she carried, the invisible battles she fought, filled me with an unbearable ache. My mind raced back to her childhood, searching for clues, for anything that could explain this hidden world of pain.

The report's mention of her suicide attempt triggered a specific memory – an incident involving her high school administration and her mother, where they had dismissed her claims of something happening to her. Could that have been the turning point? Had their disbelief pushed her further into the shadows, leaving her to grapple with her demons alone?

The weight of these questions settled heavily on my shoulders. I yearned to hold Deanna, to comfort her, to somehow erase the pain she had endured for so long. But she was struggling, and I was left grappling with the fragments of a daughter I never fully knew, the agonizing realization that I had failed to see the storm raging within her.

CHAPTER THREE
Unveiling the Past Trauma

As a father, I never thought I would find myself exploring the dark depths of child sexual abuse. But life has a way of shattering illusions in a heartbeat and forcing us to confront harsh truths. My daughter's circumstances have led me to come to terms with the clinical aspects of child sexual abuse. I believe the least I can do to help her is to better understand the profound impact of trauma and abuse on individuals.

Child sexual abuse is a distressing reality that encompasses any sexual activity involving a child without their consent or ability to give consent. This includes acts accomplished through force, threat of force, or any sexual contact between an adult and a child, regardless of deception or the child's comprehension of the situation. Even sexual contact between older and younger children can be abusive if there is a significant age, development, or size disparity, rendering the younger child incapable of giving informed consent. Such abusive acts may involve sexual penetration, sexual touching, or noncontact sexual acts such as exposure or voyeurism.

The repercussions of experiencing child sexual abuse can be far-reaching and enduring, affecting an individual's thoughts, actions, and emotions throughout their lifetime. Child sexual abuse inflicts trauma upon its victims, and it is a normal response to such abuse. Many survivors develop coping mechanisms during their childhood, which can persist into adulthood. Even when children may not fully comprehend the wrongfulness of the abuse they endure, their bodies often register the danger. It retain memories of the traumatic experiences well into their adult lives. Consequently, many women who have been victims of abuse find themselves easily triggered by reminders of their past trauma. They may experience vivid and unpleasant flashbacks, feeling as if they are reliving the distressing events.

In the face of these traumatic memories, women may adopt various ways to cope with their painful emotions. Some may develop eating disorders, misuse alcohol or drugs, or engage in self-harm. While these coping mechanisms may offer temporary relief, they often deepen feelings of isolation, depression, and anxiety. The effects of trauma can make a woman feel as though she has lost control or is on the brink of losing her sanity. She may vacillate between emotional numbness and sudden bouts of heightened alertness and panic. Often, she may not even realize that her reactions are linked to reminders of her past abuse. It is common for individuals to be unaware that childhood abuse can cast a long shadow over their lives, and they may not connect the common effects of trauma with their early experiences.

Regrettably, I didn't fully comprehend the extent of these traumatic consequences until my own daughter suffered through the horrors of child sexual abuse. In her case, it became clear that most, if not all, of these symptoms applied to her. The weight of her past experiences was crushing, and it was no wonder that she exhibited inappropriate behavior at times. Her outbursts, anger, trauma, violence, and aggression, even over seemingly trivial matters, were all rooted in the scars left by childhood sexual abuse. Witnessing her struggle firsthand has opened my eyes to the urgency of addressing this pervasive issue. This newfound understanding urges me to provide support to survivors like her.

Once I delved into Deanna's mental health history, my world began to fall apart. The weight of her struggles became apparent as I pored over the counseling report, connecting dots that had previously escaped my understanding. It was really shocking to read about the depth of what Deanna had been enduring. My heart ached for her, knowing the burden that she carried. Every page of the report revealed a new layer of pain and struggle. Depressive episodes, the haunting impact of negative experiences, sudden and bewildering behavioral changes, the suicide attempt during her high school years, unrelenting paranoia, and a profound shift in her very personality. It was as if I was peering into a dark storm that had been raging within her for far too long. The words on those pages filled me with grief as it became clear how complex Deanna's journey had been. I realized how we often don't fully comprehend the inner battles that others face, even those closest to us.

Naturally, I started reflecting on her upbringing, and my mind couldn't help but wander to the origins of her troubling habits. I delved into the research, hoping to uncover the reasons behind such behavior. It brought to mind a distressing incident she had confided in her counselor during her high school years. I recollected an event involving her mother and the apathy displayed by her high school administrators.

During her time at Madison Central High School in Madison, Mississippi, an incident of sexual abuse occurred. A male student exposed himself to Deanna, and she bravely reported it to the school. To my utter shock, the school turned a blind eye, and they took no action. It was a stroke of fate, or maybe even a higher power at work, that led me to uncover this information.

One day, while Deanna was staying with me during her vacations, she mustered the courage to share her harrowing experience. She revealed that a boy at school had exposed himself to her in the hallway, but her mother simply did not believe her. My heart sank as I processed the weight of her words. "What did you say?" I asked incredulously.

Deanna repeated, "I told my mom that a boy at school showed me his private parts while I was walking down the hall, but my mom did not believe me."

"Your own mother didn't believe you?" I asked incredulously.

"Yes, and the school didn't believe me either," she lamented, her voice heavy with despair. In that moment, frustration consumed me as I contemplated the actions of her mother and the indifference displayed by the school.

The following school day, I decided to meet with the school administrators. As I walked into their office, my mind swirled with a mix of anxiety and determination. Sitting across from the administrators, I could sense their seriousness as they confirmed Deanna's brave act of reporting the incident. However, their next words sent shockwaves through my already troubled soul. They informed me that they had reached out to Deanna's mother, but her response pierced my heart. She inexplicably refused to believe that such a traumatic event had occurred. How could she dismiss her own daughter's plea for help?

I couldn't contain my frustration any longer. Struggling to keep myself composed, I expressed my deep disappointment in their response. I reminded them of their irrefutable responsibility to thoroughly investigate any student's report, especially one as grave as this. It was a plea for justice, a plea for them to step up and protect the vulnerable. However, their reliance on a parent's statement from someone who wasn't even present during the incident left me utterly disheartened. The school administration had failed Deanna when she needed them the most. Fortunately, my words had not fallen on deaf ears. I saw a spark of action ignite within the administrators. They assured me that they would take my statement seriously, launching a thorough investigation into the matter.

Days turned into weeks as the investigation unfolded. Finally, the truth emerged, validating Deanna's courage and validating my support. The school administrators confirmed that what she had endured was indeed real. The male student responsible for her suffering was eventually expelled, albeit for a mere few days. It was a bittersweet victory, knowing that justice had been served, but my daughter had to suffer so much to get heard. The fact that Deanna continued to attend that school every day must have been excruciating for her. It likely subjected her to unimaginable psychological torture, pushing her emotions to the brink. It is no wonder that she may have contemplated suicide, given the lack of support from her parents and the authority figures she looked up to for comfort. Deanna mentioned the abuse to the appropriate authority at the school. The administration at the school contacted Deanna's mom and informed her of what Deanna had reported to them. Deanna's mom was a teacher in the same school district as Deanna's high school, which she was attending at the time. For some baffling reason, Deanna's mom refused to believe her daughter's child abuse incident. It was during one of the most vulnerable periods in Deanna's life. I can imagine how Deanna's internal self-worth could have been affected by this at this adolescent age.

The child is so dependent on their parents for comfort and protection, but when there was no comfort given to her by her mom, I just wonder how that could have psychologically affected her mentally. As I now think about her mental evaluation in which she disclosed her suicidal thoughts in high school, this situation could have triggered those thoughts.

Later, what struck me the most was the deafening silence that followed. In their final report, the school failed to reach out to me and left me in a state of confusion and frustration. It was as though they had washed their hands of the matter, with no intention of ensuring proper closure or providing me with the necessary information. It was a painful realization. Deanna's mother and the school had both failed her, turning a blind eye to the emotional scars she carried. At that time, the school made no effort to offer her any form of counseling or support, leaving her to go through the aftermath of the incident on her own.

Therefore, I am immensely grateful that Deanna trusted me enough to share this situation. I remember how, in past situations, I was the only one who believed in her when she was dealing with the crisis in her life. Despite that, at that time, I had no idea that this was a form of child sexual abuse. However, with the subsequent examination of Deanna's current behavior as it related to this terrible situation she was involved in, I somehow discovered that it is indeed a form of child sexual abuse. Once I started researching, I came to find out that it was just as dangerous mentally as any other form of child sexual abuse. Below is the definition of child sexual abuse according to "The American College of Obstetricians and Gynecologists." The definition of child sexual abuse is as follows:

"Any sexual interaction with a child who is incapable of giving consent or in a situation where consent is not possible is considered child sexual abuse. This includes sexual contact that occurs through force or the threat of force, regardless of the age of the individuals involved. It also includes any sexual interaction that takes place between an adult and a child, even when there is deceit or the youngster is unaware of the sexual nature of the engagement. Furthermore, if an older child and a younger child have substantial differences in size, age, or developmental stage, any sexual activity between them could be deemed harmful if the younger child is unable to give informed permission. Abuse can take many different forms, from non-contact behaviors like exposure or voyeurism to non-sexual stroking and penetration."

When these horrible experiences started to take a toll on Deanna's mental state, her mother actually started to feel some semblance of remorse over her actions. According to her mom, she eventually apologized to Deanna for not believing her, but what difference did it make? What if Deanna had continued suffering in silence? The predator may have continued his abuse, emboldened by the silence and Deanna's isolation. It's a chilling thought to consider, and to this day, I find it perplexing why someone would automatically assume a child is lying about such a significant incident. There must be deeper underlying reasons for Deanna's mother's lack of belief in her daughter.

When I reflect on the past, the realization leaves a bitter taste in my mouth. It seems to me that Deanna's mother had never been supportive of her daughter in her crisis situations. It's painful to admit, but this incident was not the only time she acted callously. My thoughts wander back to a dark moment from Deanna's childhood, when she was just four years old. I remember it vividly. There was an unspeakable act of child molestation committed by one of Deanna's mother's relatives. Despite the existence of medical and counseling reports that corroborated the incident, Deanna's mother refused to believe it ever happened. Even our divorce papers included a provision to protect Deanna from being unsupervised around this individual as a minor. In fact, the perpetrator's name is explicitly mentioned in the "Bench Report" attached to our divorce decree, and her mother has always had a copy of it.

During the time of the court proceedings, when our divorce was being finalized, the court system thoroughly evaluated the situation. Our case was heard by two different judges, and after years of hearings, the final decision was recorded in the bench report and divorce decree. It clearly identified the family member by name and emphasized the need to protect Deanna from this individual. If only people would take the time to read the reports, they would have no grounds for forming uninformed opinions about what Deanna suffered during those horrific encounters of childhood molestation. The evidence is there, laid out in black and white, highlighting the truth that should not be ignored or dismissed.

Yet, Deanna's mom and Deanna's mom's family turned a blind eye to that clear piece of evidence. I can hardly fathom the anguish that Deanna must have experienced when, at the tender age of four, she was told that her distressing experience was nothing more than a fabrication - a mere figment of her imagination. The torment of having family members question her truth from every angle must have been unbearable. To worsen matters, there were certain individuals within the family who harbored a deep-seated hatred toward me, individuals who I feared would project their mental animosity onto Deanna. Despite my fears, my primary concern was to protect Deanna, but I still question if I could've done more to protect her.

A parent's duty is to investigate any situation involving their precious child. In that regard, Deanna's mother failed her, but in some ways, I believe that I failed her too. Deanna's nightmare began at an early age, but I only found out about it when Deanna's mother and I were going through a painful divorce. At the time, during one of Deanna's scheduled visits, I discovered something about my little girl that turned my world upside down.

As I was changing her clothes, she casually mentioned that someone by name, had touched her inappropriately. I couldn't believe my ears. Taken aback, I asked her to repeat what she had just said. She reiterated the person's name and specified the exact location of the inappropriate touch. At that moment, I felt utterly lost, unsure of how to proceed. Without delay, I contacted our trusted pediatrician, Dr. Gearldine Chaney, whom we had relied on since Deanna's birth, and scheduled an appointment.

On the day of the appointment, I took Deanna to see Dr. Chaney, and she repeated the very same statement about this family member's actions. Concerned and seeking guidance, the pediatrician inquired whether I had discussed this matter with Deanna's mother. Regrettably, I had not yet broached the subject with her. Dr. Chaney advised me to speak with Deanna's mother first before taking any further steps. However, reaching her proved to be a challenge, as she was staying with other family members and I could only reach her through the house phone. This lack of privacy prevented me from having a transparent conversation. Faced with this problem, I pondered the situation and eventually decided to visit Deanna's mother in person, ensuring that our discussion remained confidential so as not to alarm her family. Upon arriving at the house, I approached Deanna's mother, informing her that I urgently needed to speak with her in private about something of great importance. Unfortunately, every attempt to discuss the matter privately went in vain, as one of her family members persistently inserted themselves into the conversation.

I left Deanna's mother's house, feeling a mix of confusion and frustration. I knew something significant had happened - something that needed to be addressed. So, I made my way back to Dr. Chaney's office, hoping to find some guidance and support. As I explained the situation to Dr. Chaney, the expression on her face grew grim. She assured me that she would take action and called Deanna's mom, requesting a meeting. The details of the meeting were not disclosed during the phone call because Dr. Chaney wanted to handle it delicately.

Later that evening, Deanna's mom arrived at Dr. Chaney's office, accompanied by a group of relatives. Dr. Chaney kindly asked if she could speak to Deanna's mom and me alone, as she wanted to address the matter privately. However, there was one relative whom Deanna's mom heavily relied on for guidance. This person insisted on being present in the meeting. Despite Dr. Chaney's wishes, Deanna's mom allowed this relative to join us.

Cautiously, Dr. Chaney began to discuss what Deanna had shared about the inappropriate touching by a family member. However, before she could finish, the one relative flew into a rage and refused to listen. Addressing her as the one speaking for Deanna's mom, Dr. Chaney sternly told her that she was not handling the situation wisely. She warned that if we couldn't resolve this internally, she would have to report it to the appropriate authorities. In a burst of anger, the relative sprung out of her seat and shot me a disdainful look. She then declared to Dr. Chaney that they didn't want to hear anymore and stormed out of the room, followed by Deanna's mom and the rest of the family.

Their departure left a heavy silence in the air. I couldn't help my utter disbelief at Deanna's mom and her family's reaction. After all, Dr. Chaney had been our trusted pediatrician since Deanna's birth - someone her mom respected and relied upon for all of Deanna's medical needs. This wasn't just any doctor; this was the primary caregiver who had seen Deanna through her first infant shots and had countless conversations with her mom about Deanna's well-being as a baby. Dr. Chaney had been with us through it. That's why the lack of understanding displayed by Deanna's mom left me utterly astonished. It made me question whether they were already aware of the terrible situation surrounding Deanna. The thought lingered in my mind, puzzling and deeply troubling, but I pushed it aside.

After they had left, Dr. Chaney turned to me with a serious expression. She expressed her regret but explained that she had no choice but to report the situation to the authorities. She had hoped that we, as Deanna's family, could resolve it internally without involving outside authorities or the court system. But now that hope seemed shattered. Furthermore, she shared her deep concern that if Deanna were to return to her mom's home now, she might face unhealthy pressure and questioning from her mom's family.

At that time, Deanna was still under my care. The visitation had come to an end that day, and according to the plans, I was supposed to return Deanna to her mom in the evening. However, I couldn't do so without some form of intervention and protection. Understanding the gravity of the situation, Dr. Chaney advised me to arrange a counseling session for Deanna before she could go back to her mom. Dr. Chaney promised to provide me with a list of recommended counselors who could help Deanna navigate through this traumatic experience. As I prepared to leave, she asked if I wanted her to schedule any appointments for Deanna to see. I nodded, and she proceeded to recommend a counselor along with making a phone call, and scheduling the meeting for Deanna. Grateful for her guidance, I made arrangements to meet with the counselor she had suggested.

However, as I returned home, a distressing scene awaited me. Before leaving, I had entrusted Deanna's care to a dear relative while I attended my meeting with Dr. Chaney. Little did I know the evening would unfold in a way that would leave me further seething with anger. It was later revealed to me by the relative who had been watching over Deanna that after our departure from Dr. Chaney's office, Deanna's mother and her family had paid an unexpected visit to my home. Strangely, they had never mentioned their intention to go to my house before leaving the office. The relative recounted a harrowing experience as they incessantly pounded on the door, all accompanied by a voice demanding entrance. Being unaware of who it was, my relative found herself and Deanna gripped by fear, paralyzed by the alarming commotion outside. She wisely chose not to answer the door. Thankfully, she instead decided to shield Deanna from the unknown turmoil.

When I returned home, I found the relative still visibly quite shaken, with tears streaming down her face. I immediately took her aside, explaining the bewildering situation, and tried my best to console her. She was deeply upset, burdened by the weight of being inadvertently drawn into this unsettling drama. With a heavy heart, I offered my sincerest apologies, assuring her that I had no inkling that such a chaotic episode would occur. I told her that I wasn't even aware that Deanna's mother and her family would dare to show up at my place.

It was a grievous oversight - one that would have far-reaching consequences for all involved. Therefore, after the counselor met with Deanna and presented the report to the court, the court set an emergency hearing to hear the case and render a decision that would be put in place until the case could be heard in its entirety. Following the court's decision on how to proceed, certain parameters were put in place to ensure Deanna's safety during the investigation process. However, despite the court's intervention, the animosity directed towards me by Deanna's mother continued to intensify. Ultimately, there were complications with seeing my daughter at school because of the custody agreement. Her mother's objections felt like a constant wall between us. Throughout her preschool and elementary years, there was always resistance from her mother's side whenever I tried to visit her during school hours.

One incident that sticks out vividly happened when she was just five and attending a Catholic school. Eager to see her in her classroom, I went to the office and spoke with the principal, a nun. The news that I received wasn't what I expected. The nun informed me that Deanna's mom had said I wasn't allowed to visit. Shocked, I demanded to see anything in writing that restricted my right to see my daughter.

The nun asked me to wait and said she'd be back shortly. While I waited outside her office, I overheard a phone conversation. The nun was asking Deanna's mom why I couldn't visit and if there was any legal documentation, like a court order, preventing my presence. I couldn't hear the response, but thankfully, the head nun soon emerged with a change of heart. I was allowed to see Deanna in her classroom!

We had a wonderful visit, and it brightened up both my day and my daughter's.

Figure 6: Me, attending an afterschool program with Deanna at the Catholic School.

Of course, the challenges continued, but I never gave up on being involved in Deanna's education. I kept visiting her at every school and even got involved with the parent associations. The head nun and I developed a friendship during Deanna's time at the Catholic school, and I participated in some school activities when the students weren't present. My dedication to her education stayed strong right until I dropped her off at the University of Mississippi (Ole Miss), where she attended and received her college degree.

My daughter had grown up into a strong, beautiful woman. In the aftermath of her trauma, I had tried my best to help her climb her way out of that hell. Yet, the weight of these events burdened my thoughts day after day, year after year. I couldn't help but ruminate on how Deanna's mother and I could have navigated this situation differently.

How could I have shielded our daughter from the harsh realities of the court system? Unbridled resentment brewed within me, particularly toward that one relative of Deanna's mom who had inflicted harm upon her. Had it not been for the interference of Deanna's mom's family, this relative's name wouldn't have even appeared in our divorce decree.

Despite every action I took, two questions persistently echoed in my mind, even to this day. Firstly, were Deanna's family members aware of the disturbing incidents that unfolded within their own household concerning Deanna before she confided in me and Dr. Chaney? It seemed as though Deanna's mom and her family were in a state of denial, unwilling to listen to Dr. Chaney's professional guidance or heed Deanna's words. I often wondered if Deanna had already shared these same painful truths with her mother and her family.

The second question that plagued me was whether I had handled the situation appropriately. If not, what could I have done differently? I pondered endlessly on how Deanna's mom and I could have united, working together to protect our precious daughter. Sometimes, I wondered if I should have simply ignored the weight of Deanna's revelation, pretending as if she had never uttered those words. It gnawed at me, causing immense turmoil, especially when I occasionally crossed paths with Deanna's mom.

As a father, I reacted instinctively to my daughter's distressing disclosure, but her family held animosity toward me for fiercely safeguarding her. I felt isolated, like a lone castaway on an island. Nevertheless, I want to make one thing clear: I cared little for the opinions of Deanna's mom's family; my commitment was to protect my daughter at any cost. It was my duty as her father, and I waged this battle alone, confiding in only my parents, who had witnessed the courtroom hearings where the allegations of child trauma inflicted upon Deanna by one of her mom's relatives were discussed. The emotional toll of these events was immeasurable.

At the same time, it pains me to think how Deanna never received justice. The family member who inflicted such trauma upon her has been allowed to carry on with their life as if nothing ever happened. Meanwhile, Deanna continues to suffer from the deep wounds inflicted upon her. The denial and concealment of what happened to her was a grave mistake. Both her mother and I failed Deanna in that regard. I should have persisted in fighting for justice, making sure she was aware as she grew older. However, I couldn't bear the thought of causing a rift between Deanna and the ones she loved, particularly her mother. Little did I know the extent of the damage that had been done to her, and now I am determined to ensure that she no longer bears this burden alone.

Deanna still has a long journey ahead of her, filled with healing and recovery from the trauma of her childhood. It is crucial to understand that none of this is her fault. The blame lies solely with the perpetrator and those who prioritized protecting them over Deanna's mental well-being. The individual who shielded the perpetrator showed a complete disregard for Deanna's suffering.

As I write this book, I find myself grappling with a pressing question: how can I broach this sensitive topic with Deanna? It seems that I am the only one who truly believes in her - who has stood by her side throughout these years of turmoil.

Sometimes, it felt like it was just Deanna and me against the world as I fought to protect her. The most challenging time was during the court proceedings, where I had to defend her against those who doubted her and me regarding the experiences of sexual abuse that she was subjected to by a relative on her mother's side. It was a tough period that took a toll on my mental well-being as well.

Before it was finally resolved in the divorce papers on how we were going to protect Deanna, Deanna's mom and I spent nearly three years dealing with this circumstance and our divorce through the legal system. I think the main reason it took so long was that Deanna's mother and her family absolutely wanted our final divorce decree to exclude the relative's name. I firmly feel that several people felt the lengthy procedure would cause me to collapse. Yes, I did experience some challenging days. But in order to obtain the solace I wanted, I had to go well beyond my comfort zone.

During these trying times, I stumbled upon a passage in the Bible that provided me with the strength and comfort I needed to continue fighting for Deanna. Though I'm not sure how I found it, this passage became a source of inspiration and support for me. It was from the King James Version, Psalm 64:

"Hear my voice, O God, in my prayer: preserve my life from fear of the enemy. Hide me from the secret counsel of the wicked, from the insurrection of the workers of iniquity. They sharpen their tongues like swords and bend their bows to shoot their arrows, even bitter words. They shoot at the innocent in secret, without any fear. They encourage themselves in evil schemes, discussing how to set traps without being seen. They search for wrongdoing and investigate diligently, their thoughts and hearts being deeply cunning. However, God will strike them with an arrow, suddenly causing them harm. Their own words will come back to haunt them, and all who witness their downfall will flee. All people will fear and acknowledge the work of God, wisely considering His actions. The righteous will rejoice in the Lord, trusting in Him, and those with pure hearts will give glory to Him."

If there is anyone out there going through a situation similar to what Deanna and I have endured, I implore you not to let others divert your attention from the crux of the matter. It's disheartening to witness how those who seek to protect the wrongdoer employ cunning tactics to shift our focus onto unrelated matters. As we are all in this together, let me share my unwavering belief: God has a way of exposing those who believe they have escaped the consequences of their deceitful actions.

This book would not exist had it not been for the harrowing ordeal that Deanna faced within the confines of the legal system. It is through tragedy that veiled truths are brought to light, revealing what we once thought was hidden. As long as there is breath in my body, I will stand by my girls. I will be their unyielding anchor in the face of storms, and it is during these trying times that the darkest secrets are unveiled, bringing to the surface the very individuals who believed they had evaded justice. In these moments, God, in His divine wisdom, exposes those who refuse to repent, those who bear the weight of true guilt. There is an old saying etched deep within the annals of time: "The truth will come to light." And in this case, it holds true. God has paved the way for the revelation of those who thought their deceitful acts against the vulnerable would forever remain concealed.

So, if you find yourself grappling with a similar situation, take solace in the fact that you are not alone. Trust in the power of truth and the eventual unmasking of those who have wronged you. In the end, justice prevails, and the light of truth will shine brightly upon the darkness of deceit.

CHAPTER FOUR
The Protective Sister's Dilemma

Deanna is a kind soul, full of love and fierce protectiveness for those she cares about. Her warmth radiated outwards, creating a safe place for those around her. Yet, here she was, having done something that seemed so out of character. Looking back, anyone can see that it all stemmed from her love for her little sister, Mia. Throughout the crisis, she must have felt that the system had failed Mia, leaving her vulnerable and in need of support. Deanna found herself at a loss, unsure of how to navigate this daunting situation.

The catalyst for Deanna's anger was the shocking sight of Mia's ex-boyfriend showing up uninvited at their home. This wasn't the first time. This was the same person who had previously been warned by the Jackson Police Department to stay away from them, yet here he was, a constant threat looming over their lives.

On that fateful day, an altercation ensued between Deanna and Mia's ex-boyfriend, fueling Deanna's already simmering rage. It seemed as though those in positions of authority had repeatedly let her down, leaving her feeling helpless and abandoned.

Deanna must have felt a familiar sting of betrayal. Authority figures had let them down before. Her own mother, during her childhood abuse, had refused to believe her pleas. Deanna held a series of crushed hopes and broken trust, shattered by those who were supposed to be her support system. The counselor's report that I received on November 30th spoke of these inner demons; it was a constant battle Deanna fought. With a mind clouded by emotional turmoil, Deanna made a choice, the worst one of her life.

The shocking turn of events didn't just impact Deanna; it had a profound effect on Mia as well. Following the incident, Mia felt an urgent need to escape the toxic environment that surrounded her, particularly with her ex-boyfriend lingering dangerously close. With this in mind, Mia made the difficult decision to leave Jackson, seeking refuge with her grandmother in the serene city of New Orleans, Louisiana.

In the aftermath of that dreadful day when Deanna was arrested for the shooting, Mia found herself grappling with a multitude of difficult emotions. Overwhelmed by guilt, she couldn't help but blame herself for the tragic outcome. It was heartbreaking to witness Mia carry this burden. As Mia's confidant and source of comfort, I constantly reminded her that this devastating situation was not her fault. Life has a way of unfolding in ways beyond our control, and sometimes, unfortunate events are simply destined to occur. Whenever her thoughts were plagued by doubts, I assured Mia that Deanna loved her deeply, just as I knew Mia loved her sister with all her heart.

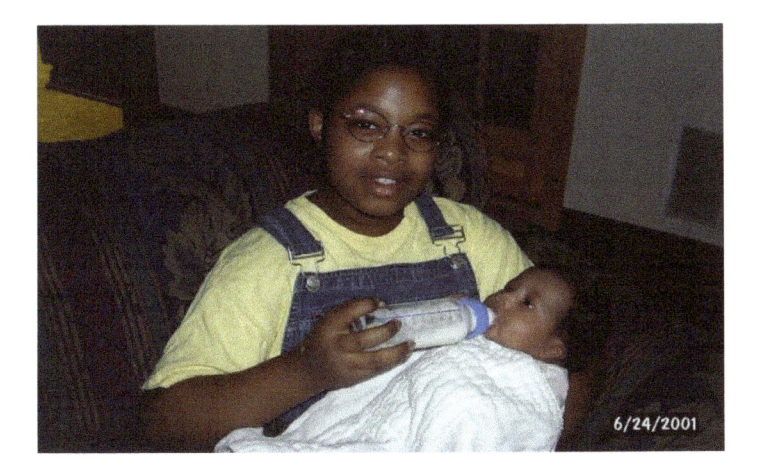

Figure 7: Deanna feeding Mia a bottle of Milk at an early age.

This whole situation brought back a flood of memories that reflected the unwavering protectiveness Deanna had always felt for Mia. It was like a mother hen guarding her chick. I can still picture Deanna so vividly, holding a newborn Mia just days after she entered the world. The tiny bundle cradled in Deanna's arms, the gentle way she fed Mia one of her first bottles of milk – the scene is permanently marked in my mind. Time had stolen away the years, leaving behind two grown women. However, the age gap of ten years never seemed to matter, and their bond remained unbreakable.

In the depths of my reflection, my mind wandered back to 2008, a year that held significance for me as the author of a book titled "Mississippi's Uncovered Glory." Within the pages of that book, I delved into the profound relationship between Deanna and Mia. On page 125, I had penned words that now stirred strong emotions within me. I wrote: "When my oldest daughter, Deanna, was born, that was one of the most fulfilling and happy days of my life. Deanna's mom had not only delivered a new breathing baby, but she had put some life back into my body. There is no way that I could ever repay Deanna's mom for what she gave me in the month of September 1991. After Deanna was born, I thought about her every day. I did not want her to feel all the emptiness that I had felt over the years of not having a sibling. In May 2001, Deanna's little sister was born. My feelings and thoughts went to Deanna and Mia after Mia's birth. I knew that they would be there to help support, love, and protect each other as they took the journey through this world. Each time I see Mia's mom, I am truly thankful for her."

My reflections on my daughters evoke memories of my own adolescence, overshadowed by the tragic loss of my only brother to a football-related brain injury when he was just 19 years old. For a considerable time, this loss weighed heavily on my heart, serving as a constant burden that I carried with me. However, the arrival of Deanna into my life marked a significant turning point, offering solace and a renewed sense of purpose.

In this journey called life, each of us is endowed with a purpose; some of us are aware of it, while others are still searching for their calling. Deanna, with her selfless spirit, had always strived to make a positive impact on those around her. Her life touched many, leaving a trail of kindness in its wake. However, fate can be a cruel hand. I hold steadfast in my belief that much of what unfolds in our lives is part of a divine plan orchestrated by a higher power. It is no coincidence that the unfortunate incident involving Deanna shooting at Mia's ex-boyfriend came to pass. It was destined to happen, but this does not absolve us of the choices we make along the way, for we possess the power to shape the course of our own existence. In the face of darkness, God has a way of illuminating the truth, revealing what some may have hoped would remain buried in shadows. The weight of this situation took an immense toll on Deanna, leaving her profoundly affected by the repercussions of her actions.

The decision to pursue an open plea agreement was made after careful consideration and consultation with both Deanna and her attorney. Among the various options available, it was deemed the most favorable choice. The circumstances surrounding the case left no doubt as to whether Deanna was involved in the shooting, as there was indeed someone present in the house during the incident.

Deanna's motivation for her actions stemmed from the harm inflicted upon Mia and herself, by Mia's ex-boyfriend. While I thought it was likely that the jury would sympathize with her situation, it is important to acknowledge that she was still held accountable for her actions. Guilt weighed heavily upon her as she grappled with the consequences of her choices. The best deal offered by the District Attorney's office entailed a sentence of 15 years on one charge and 5 years on another charge.

Amidst the legal proceedings, one of the gravest concerns surrounding Deanna's situation was the fact that four bullets had struck the house, endangering the innocent life of Mia's ex-boyfriend's grandmother. She was an unwitting bystander, caught in the crossfire of a situation she had no part in. It is a blessing that no further harm befell anyone else within the confines of that house, and for that, we offer our gratitude to a higher power.

While writing this book, a heavy question settled on me: how would I talk to Deanna about her childhood trauma? Along this journey, it became apparent to me that I may be the only person capable of discussing these matters with her, as I am the sole individual privy to the reports from the doctor and counselor. Unfortunately, I discovered later that her mom had refused to read these reports in the past, and they had been securely filed in a sealed court system.

However, it is worth noting that the name of the perpetrator is directly identified in Deanna's mother's "Bench Report," which is attached to our divorce decree. Her mother has always had a copy of this report.

For those who have not read these reports, their opinions on the harrowing experiences Deanna endured at the hands of her mother's relative hold little weight. The reports contained the professional assessments of trained therapists and medical professionals. These were the people who had listened to Deanna's story, examined the evidence, and reached a clear conclusion: Deanna had been abused. Without this knowledge, how could anyone truly understand the trauma she carried and the impact it had on her life? Forming an opinion based on speculation or hearsay was not only insensitive, and it was a disservice to Deanna and the truth.

I empathize with anyone going through this ordeal. To anyone else currently facing circumstances similar to Deanna's and mine, I implore you not to let others sidetrack you from addressing the main issues. It is all too common for those attempting to shield the perpetrator to employ tactics aimed at diverting your attention away from reality. Stay resolute in seeking justice and support, for your experiences and struggles deserve to be acknowledged and addressed with the utmost care and consideration.

During the open plea process, the judge provides an opportunity for the defendant to express remorse either to the court or to the victims involved. Additionally, the defendant is allowed to have individuals speak on their behalf, sharing any relevant information that can help the judge understand their character as a person. It is hoped that the defendant's good character will play a significant role in the judge's determination of the appropriate sentencing.

It is important to note that the open plea opportunity is not a time for the defendant to place blame. Instead, it is an opportunity for them to acknowledge their guilt and express remorse for the complex circumstances surrounding the crime. The focus should be on conveying to the judge that the behavior exhibited is not representative of their normal character. If there is any need for blame to be presented, it is the responsibility of the defendant's attorney to do so, presenting any mitigating circumstances that may have contributed to the situation.

Mitigating circumstances are factors that can lessen the severity or culpability of a criminal act. These can include the defendant's age, extreme mental or emotional disturbance at the time of the crime, mental retardation, or a lack of a prior criminal record. These circumstances can be presented by the defendant's attorney to provide a more comprehensive understanding of the defendant's situation.

It is important to remember that the judge has the authority to accept or reject the plea agreement. The judge will consider the proposed disposition and whether it is just. If the plea agreement is accepted, the judge will inform the defendant of the imposed sentence. If the plea agreement is rejected, the judge will provide the opportunity for the defendant to withdraw their plea.

The plea-bargaining process is a private one, although victims' rights groups are increasingly recognized and may have input in the process. The details of a plea bargain are typically not made public until they are announced in court. The judge's role is to ensure that the plea agreement is fair and just, considering all relevant factors before making a decision.

Deanna's attorney and I discussed what could be said during the open plea, and he emphasized that we could focus on highlighting positive aspects of her character. We could discuss her personal relationships and how the individuals who would be speaking on her behalf relate to her. He further emphasized that we should reflect on her childhood and adolescent years. However, he made it clear that the open plea is not a time for Deanna to place blame or make excuses for her actions. By taking the open plea, Deanna is already acknowledging her guilt and taking responsibility for her own actions without blaming anyone else.

I relayed this information to the individuals who would be speaking on Deanna's behalf during the open plea hearing. Deanna provided me with a list of people she wanted to ensure were present:

- Deanna's Mom: I informed Deanna's mom about the opportunity to speak on her behalf during the open plea hearing.

- Me, her Dad: As her father, it was important for me to be present and speak about Deanna's character and personal growth.

- Deanna's grandmother, Etherlene Gentry, is on her dad's side of the family. Deanna wanted her grandmother to share insights into her upbringing and the values she instilled in her.

- Dr. Safiya Omari, Chief of Staff at the City of Jackson, MS: Deanna worked for Dr. Omari during her time at the City of Jackson, and she wanted Dr. Omari to speak about her professional character and work ethic.

- Kendra Redding, a registered nurse: Kendra has been Deanna's long-time friend, having attended high school together at Madison Central High School and being roommates during college at the University of Mississippi (Ole Miss). She has remained Deanna's closest friend and confidant throughout adulthood.

Deanna chose these individuals to provide a comprehensive picture of her character and the positive impact she has had on those around her. Their testimonies would shed light on her upbringing, personal relationships, and professional endeavors, ultimately contributing to the judge's understanding of who Deanna is as a person.

Deanna's open plea was approaching, and I wrestled with a difficult decision. Should I speak about the childhood trauma Deanna had endured? This secret, this burden she carried, felt crucial to understanding who she was. But there was a complication. Deanna's attorney had represented her mother during our divorce. Back then and up until that moment, I was unsure of his thoughts about Deanna's childhood abuse. In the aftermath of that bitter memory, I found myself wondering: Could I trust him to handle this sensitive information with the empathy it deserved? Years had passed, and we had interacted professionally since then, but the past remained a shadow as we never talked openly about that. I couldn't help my uncertainty. Deanna's story needed to be told, but I was a little skeptical about talking about Deanna's traumatic past with him.

Despite my initial uncertainty, I requested a meeting with Deanna's attorney before the open plea trial to discuss the possibility of mentioning her childhood trauma. I explained to him that I was unsure if Deanna had any recollection of the incidents and that we had never discussed it specifically. I provided him with the details of both incidents, including the one with her mother's relative and the incident that occurred during her high school years.

To my surprise, Deanna's attorney did not hesitate to advise me to mention these incidents during the open plea hearing. I reiterated that I had never spoken to Deanna about the child molestation involving her mother's relative. However, he explained that it was necessary for her to hear it as it needed to be mentioned in the open court. Despite my initial concerns, his response left me feeling more comfortable about addressing these sensitive topics during Deanna's open plea trial.

After leaving the meeting with Deanna's attorney, I felt a mix of emotions. There was a sense of relief and gratitude that he had given me the green light to discuss the sensitive incidents surrounding her childhood trauma. At the same time, I couldn't help but feel a wave of concern for Deanna. Putting all my doubts aside, I started to make the phone calls to each individual on Deanna's list of speakers. As I spoke with each person, I explained the purpose of the upcoming hearing. And the significance of their presence. I wanted them to understand just how important it was for them to speak on Deanna's behalf.

As I pondered over what to say at Deanna's open plea hearing, I felt the weight of the sensitive information I needed to share. I decided it was best to speak with Deanna's mom face-to-face. So, I called her up and arranged a meeting at my home, where I reside with my wife. My wife had met Deanna's mom a couple of years ago when this terrible incident concerning Deanna first occurred. My wife was aware of the upcoming trial, and she welcomed Deanna's mom into our home. However, at this time, my wife had no idea of the past childhood trauma that Deanna had encountered. It was still a little difficult for me to share this information. For some reason, I felt ashamed of Deanna, and I was not sure why I felt that way. Therefore, when Deanna's mom arrived, I gently broached the subject, explaining that I had just discussed matters with Deanna's attorney.

I handed her copies of Deanna's medical records and information on the symptoms of untreated adult trauma stemming from child molestation. Alongside, I provided our divorce decree, which pointed to a relative of hers as the perpetrator of Deanna's childhood trauma.

To my surprise, Deanna's mom immediately dismissed the notion, claiming it couldn't have happened because Deanna never mentioned it. I was taken aback and asked, "Did you ask her about it?" She hesitated before admitting that she hadn't. When she added that Deanna was never alone with the relative, I couldn't help but feel a pang of frustration.

I reflected on the times when Deanna's grandmother, on her mom's side, cared for her during the day while her mom was teaching. I remembered picking Deanna up for visits when the relative was present. This was before the time Deanna had disclosed what her mom's relative had done to her. It struck me that Deanna's mom's certainty wasn't based on firsthand knowledge. At that moment, my thoughts toward her became somewhat disheartened. I was thinking that I didn't have time to tell her what had happened and that she had already programmed her mind to believe it didn't happen. I didn't want to go through all of that again and expend a lot of emotional energy on telling someone who has been doubting her for years the specifics of how my young girl was molested. I had no desire to try and persuade her of anything.

However, as I continued to express my concerns, it became apparent that Deanna's mom wasn't swaying. I couldn't help but recall the past, when Deanna had confided in her about the abuse during high school, only to face disbelief.

I confronted her gently, reminding her of those times, to which she admitted she had apologized to Deanna later. But her curiosity lingered, and she pressed me for details about what Deanna had shared regarding the incident with the relative.

Feeling uneasy, I evaded the question, stating, "I don't want to talk about that now. I'm just here to inform you of what I plan to say at Deanna's hearing." My sole aim, I stressed, was to advocate for Deanna's well-being - to sway the court toward compassion and leniency.

I assured her that I had already discussed my intentions with Deanna's attorney, who raised no objections to mentioning her childhood traumas. Yet, her unexpected query caught me off guard: "Who brought up the idea?"

Anxiously, I replied, "What does it matter?" But she insisted on knowing, so I reluctantly admitted, "I brought it up and discussed it with him."

Her insistence seemed to probe deeper, making me feel vulnerable and uneasy.

Our conversation ended on a strange note as she repeated the inquiry, "So, you brought up the idea?"

I answered curtly, "Yes."

Reflecting on the exchange with Deanna's mom, I realized the weight of the attorney-client relationship. Everything shared between the client and attorney remained strictly confidential. I understood that Deanna's current attorney had previously represented her mom in our divorce proceedings and in court hearings involving the relative accused of molesting Deanna as a toddler.

As I mulled over this, a twinge of curiosity crept in—was Deanna's mom hiding something from me all these years? Despite the nagging curiosity, I knew my focus had to remain on Deanna's impending trial.

The night before Deanna's open plea hearing, Deanna's mom reached out to me, pleading with me to remain silent on the child abuse incidents. However, I stood firm, believing the court needed to understand Deanna's past struggles. I explained to her, "This trial is about Deanna, not you. She's faced numerous disappointments in her life, and the court needs to comprehend every aspect that could influence her sentencing."

Despite her pleas, I reiterated my stance, emphasizing that the court needed to grasp the full extent of Deanna's mental state. I assured her, "I'm going to address how both of us failed Deanna, not just you."

As I hung up the phone, her words lingered in my mind. She couldn't sway me because I had made up my mind to speak for Deanna's truth. Perhaps that was the longest and the most restless night of my life. However, as I found myself drifting off to sleep, I just had one thought in my mind: *I'll support Deanna through thick and thin!*

CHAPTER FIVE
Confronting the Legal System

There are moments in life that shape our very existence, defining who we are and what we become. For me, that moment arrived on the 5th of December, a day etched in my memory forever. It was the day of the trial, and the courtroom was filled with anticipation as we gathered for the opening plea hearing.

As the judge took his seat, he called upon Deanna's attorney and the assistant district attorney representing the state of Mississippi to confirm their readiness to proceed. Both parties answered in the affirmative, signaling that the time had come to unveil the case before us. The district attorney would be the first to present the background of the case against Deanna, and the judge, acknowledging this, granted permission to proceed.

With a clear voice, the district attorney laid out the entirety of the case, revealing that they had no specific punishment recommendation at this time. He also stated that the state had no objections to an open plea hearing. The judge, seeking clarity, asked if any evidence would be presented during this hearing. The district attorney informed us that they had one witness lined up—a significant figure in the story. It was the grandmother of Mia's ex-boyfriend, who had been present in the house when the shooting occurred.

This revelation caught me off guard, and I found myself scanning the room, searching for the unfamiliar face of this lady. My eyes darted from one person to another, but there was no indication that anyone would step forward to speak. With the judge's prompt, it was time for the district attorney to make their move. Looking past me, they called upon the grandmother of Mia's ex-boyfriend to take the stand.

As the district attorney's words hung in the air, a wave of numbness washed over me, causing my heart to sink and my stomach to twist in agony. Fear enveloped my entire being, its icy grip rendering me motionless. It was a shocking revelation that the innocent lady who had been present in the house during the fateful shooting would now take the stand. I had read the police report detailing her interview, where she had expressed her fear upon hearing the shots and promptly called 911 to report the incident. In that instant, I knew that we were facing an uphill battle. The open plea trial we had opted for seemed to be leading us down a treacherous path, devoid of any hope for leniency from the court. The grandmother's impending testimony only added to our mounting difficulties.

As she approached the podium, a rush of thoughts flooded my mind. Had we made the right decision? I was tormented by my own doubt as I questioned the wisdom of our chosen path. I had never anticipated that Mia's ex-boyfriend's grandmother would be the one to speak. In my mind, if anyone were to testify from the district attorney's side, it would have been Mia's ex-boyfriend himself. His involvement in Deanna's actions that day could have been addressed by her attorney, shedding light on the negative aspects of his role.

When the District attorney witness for the state approached the podium, a hushed anticipation settled over the entire courtroom. The air was thick with tension, and all eyes were fixed upon her. And then, with her first statement, everything changed.

"Your honor," she began, "I believe I may belong on the other side, for I am here to request compassion and leniency for Deanna."

Those words hit me like a bolt of lightning, and my heart plummeted from surprise. It was a sudden shift, transforming the atmosphere from one of fear and uncertainty to a tender sense of hope. I hadn't expected such a response.

She went on to explain that everyone makes mistakes, acknowledging that Deanna must have been carrying a burden at the time of the incident. With genuine sincerity, she expressed her belief that if Deanna was Mia's sister, she had to be a sweet and kind-hearted young lady, just like Mia herself. Although she had never met Deanna before, she implored the court to show her leniency and compassion.

In that moment, as I watched Mia's ex-boyfriend's grandmother speaking, a wave of relief washed over me. It was the first time I had laid eyes on her, yet her unexpected plea for understanding lifted some of the immense weight that had been pressing down upon me. The anticipated stress seemed to dissipate as her response was a twist in the tale that none of us had foreseen.

As she took her seat right behind me in the courtroom, I turned around and silently mouthed the words "Thank you." I wasn't sure if she knew who I was, but she quietly responded, "I was just telling the truth." Her simple words resonated deeply within me, and I couldn't express enough gratitude for the impact she had on me in that moment at the podium.

I realized that her statement might not necessarily sway the court's final decision in Deanna's case. However, it certainly wouldn't negatively influence the court's decision-making process. That in itself was a positive outcome, and all we needed at that moment was from any of the state's witnesses. It was a small instance of positivity.

The judge then turned to the District attorney and inquired if there were any further witnesses that the state wished to present at that time. The District attorney informed the judge that they had no other witnesses or additional evidence to present at that moment. With that, the chapter of witness testimonies came to a close, leaving us to await the next phase of the trial.

Proceeding, the judge turned to Deanna's attorney and stated, "You may proceed with your case." With the judge's permission, Deanna's attorney went on to present character witnesses on her behalf. He specifically requested that Dr. Omari speak first. I had just recently learned that she was a licensed psychologist on the day prior to her speaking. Dr. Omari took the stand, introducing herself as a licensed psychologist and the chief of staff for the city of Jackson, Mississippi.

Dr. Omari described Deanna's congenial personality and the positive image she had portrayed while working in the city. However, it was her next statement that caught me completely off guard. Dr. Omari revealed that, through years of observing Deanna's behavior, she had come to the conclusion that Deanna had experienced significant childhood trauma. She explained that Deanna's behavior changes had signaled to her that she carried the weight of a painful past.

I was taken aback by Dr. Omari's remarks. I had no idea that someone had made such a determination about Deanna's past. The revelation left me stunned, and my mind struggled to process this new information. It was as if a fog had settled over my thoughts, momentarily numbing my ability to fully comprehend the gravity of what had just been revealed.

Once Dr. Omari took her seat, Deanna's attorney summoned her longtime companion, Kendra Redding, to speak on Deanna's behalf. Kendra, a well-respected registered nurse who has been a steadfast friend of Deanna's for many years, eloquently shared anecdotes and praised Deanna's personal achievements. She emphasized Deanna's unwavering support throughout their lives and commended her professionalism in her career.

After Kendra concluded her testimony and returned to her seat, it was time for Deanna's grandmother, my mother, to address the court. At 88 years old, she relied on a walker and had difficulty moving around. Assisting her to rise and make her way to the podium, the courtroom fell silent, all eyes fixed upon her as she took each step. The court acknowledged her presence, and the attorney nodded, giving her the signal to speak. Emotions overwhelmed her, making it challenging for her to find her voice. Tears welled up in her eyes as she struggled to convey her thoughts. With great effort, she managed to express that Deanna had been her lifeline and caretaker for the past two years. Though her words were few, the depth of her love and gratitude for Deanna was visible in the courtroom.

The powerful silence that enveloped the room during her brief testimony spoke volumes. After helping my mother back to her seat, the attorney motioned for Deanna's mom to approach the podium. Deanna's mom introduced herself and began to speak about the support that Deanna had always provided her. She recounted how Deanna had been by her side during the momentous occasion of receiving her National Board Certification for teaching in the state of Mississippi. Emotion filled her voice as she declared Deanna to be her best friend. In a heartfelt gesture, Deanna's mom read aloud a letter from one of Deanna's high school teachers, praising Deanna's outstanding performance as a student. The words of admiration and recognition rang through the courtroom, further highlighting Deanna's positive qualities and potential.

Deanna's mom concluded her speech by requesting that the court allow Deanna to continue her punishment under house arrest, as she had been doing for the past two years, wearing an ankle monitor. It was a plea for mercy and an acknowledgment of the progress Deanna had made during her time under house arrest. Having conveyed her message, Deanna's mom returned to her seat.

After what felt like an eternity, Deanna's attorney motioned for me to come to the podium. As I stood there, time seemed to suspend itself in the hushed courtroom. My steps to the podium felt uneasy, as if each footfall echoed with the weight of the moment. Here I was, preparing to plead for understanding and leniency for my beloved daughter, Deanna. I knew the gravity of her actions, yet I yearned for the court to see beyond the surface to understand the essence of the person she truly was.

With a heart burdened with both remorse and determination, I addressed the court, "Thank you. Thank you for allowing me to speak on behalf of my daughter." The words spilled forth, an apology tinged with love and regret. "I'm deeply sorry for what Deanna has done, especially to Mia's ex-boyfriend's grandmother."

My gaze shifted to Deanna, my voice catching with emotion. "Deanna, sweetheart, you know how much I love you. Thank you for all you've done for me." Each word felt heavy with the weight of our shared history, our struggles, and our triumphs.

Gathering my thoughts, I shared a deeply personal story with the court. I spoke of the profound impact my brother's passing had on me when I was just 18 years old - how it had left me feeling as though I had given up on life. "When Deanna was born in 1991, she gave me life back," I confessed, the memories flooding back with bittersweet intensity.

With a voice laden with emotion, I recounted the countless ways in which Deanna had touched the lives of others, the selfless acts of kindness and support she had offered. I spoke of her role as a devoted caregiver for my mother, emphasizing the love and dedication that she had shown over the past two years. While I didn't seek to excuse her actions, I acknowledged that she had made a poor choice.

Amidst the tender reminiscences, there lay the harsh reality of our failings as parents. "We failed her," I admitted, my voice thick with regret. "Her mom and I failed to recognize her needs to get her the help that she deserved." I did not shy away from acknowledging our shortcomings, our blindness to Deanna's silent struggles, and our neglect in seeking the professional guidance she so desperately required.

My voice wavered as I delved into the childhood sexual abuse she had endured at the hands of a family member just as a toddler. I discussed the impact it had on her personality and actions in adulthood. I described her experiences of child molestation and the lack of support and belief she received from her own mother. I referenced information from the CDC and AACAP, painting a vivid picture of the long-term effects of childhood molestation if left untreated. I made a heartfelt plea for the court to recognize the urgent need for Deanna to receive help in coping with the myriad of challenges she faced.

However, my narrative did not end with our familial failings. I cast a wider net, implicating the educational system that had turned a blind eye to Deanna's suffering and the community that had failed to offer solace and support when she needed it most. In detailing the sexual abuse Deanna endured during her high school years, I implored the court to recognize the systemic failures that had compounded her pain and contributed to her current predicament. Furthermore, I continued to make a plea for her punishment to be confined to an institution that could address the deep-rooted issues she had faced. I shared that I had already researched facilities that were willing to provide her with the necessary rehabilitation treatment.

In a final plea, I spoke of Deanna's involvement with the Department of Public Safety, her supportive role in her sister Mia's life, and her impactful conversations with influential figures. I described her boundless love and care for her grandmother, recounting the time that she had saved her life.

As I concluded my impassioned plea, I turned once more to the judge, my voice quavering with emotion. I begged for compassion, for understanding, for a sentence that would prioritize Deanna's rehabilitation over punitive measures. And as the weight of my words hung in the air, the judge offered a subtle nod of acknowledgment, and dismissed me by saying, "You are welcome."

The weight of the moment lingered in the air, and I could only hope that my heartfelt plea had reached the hearts of those who held Deanna's fate in their hands.

As I returned to my seat, the courtroom brimmed with tension. Each passing moment was pregnant with anticipation. Deanna's attorney beckoned her forward, and as she approached the podium, a sudden wail pierced the air. Deanna's mother erupted into anguished cries and erratic movements. Stunned and unsure, I sat beside her, grappling with the shock of her outburst, unsure how to calm her tumultuous emotions. The seconds stretched on, and her distress continued, leaving me at a loss for words. Her cries reverberated through the room. Acting on instinct, I tentatively reached out, gently placing a comforting hand on her shoulder, hoping to offer some solace. But my mind raced with worry, fretting over the potential impact of her breakdown on Deanna's sentencing. Would the judge view this as a negative influence on the proceedings?

Moments later, a bailiff approached with instructions from the judge, requesting that Deanna's mother leave the courtroom. I followed them out, filled with worry and uncertainty, ensuring that she was alright. As the bailiff escorted her to a seat outside the courtroom, I leaned in as the bailiff whispered to me to tell Deanna's mom not to blame herself for anything. So I repeated to her what the bailiff had said to me.

Once I was certain that she had settled, I hurriedly returned to the courtroom to witness Deanna addressing the court. Her voice trembled with emotion as tears streamed down her cheeks, expressing deep remorse for her actions. I listened as she offered apologies to Mia's ex-boyfriend, the victim, and Mia's ex-boyfriend's grandmother, acknowledging the ordeal that they had been through.

Just as I focused on Deanna's heartfelt words, her mother reentered the courtroom and took her seat. However, the judge intervened, informing Deanna's mother that she would have to leave and could not return due to her outburst. Deanna's mother left the courtroom, and Deanna concluded her statement, expressing gratitude to the judge for allowing her to address the court on her behalf.

Following Deanna's heartfelt expression, it was her attorney's turn to advocate on her behalf, seeking the judge's leniency in determining the sentence. In the depths of my heart, I had grappled with the realization that Deanna would likely face some form of incarceration due to the severity of the situation. Yet, a fervent hope and prayer lingered within me, desiring a sentence shorter than the ominous offer presented by the District attorney prior to the trial. The weight of the impending judgment loomed heavily upon us all. Even after the favorable proceedings of the court trial, I knew that the judge's decision could potentially impose a harsher sentence that would be unappealable.

However, as Deanna's attorney delved into the mitigating circumstances of the case, he implored the court to consider the array of statements presented on Deanna's behalf. He emphasized the need to recognize Deanna's positive character, stressing that a single incident could not define her as a person. The attorney shed light on the history of her mental health issues revealed in her evaluation and the harrowing experiences of child molestation that she had endured during her formative years. With a sense of finality, he acknowledged to the judge that this was the entirety of the case they would present on behalf of Deanna.

To my surprise, the judge swiftly transitioned into the sentencing phase of the case. My hopes hung in a delicate balance, yearning for a sentence less severe than the Assistant District attorney's previous offer of 20 years to serve for both charges. The gravity of the situation weighed heavily on my heart. She had discharged a weapon, and the repercussions had led to four bullets striking the house of an innocent individual. With a steadfast resolve, I steeled myself to hear the judge's ruling.

I held my breath as the judge looked directly at me. "The punishment required for this matter exceeds that of a habilitation facility. I understand your compassion for your daughter; it's a battle you're fighting." His words resonated with solemn authority. "I comprehend the emotions you are contending with, for I have walked that path before," he continued, acknowledging the depth of the turmoil I was experiencing. "I also recognize the childhood trauma that she has endured, but as an adult, she holds the responsibility to seek help for herself and address her issues." His words carried an undercurrent of gravity, instilling a sense of apprehension within me.

With a heavy heart, I braced myself as the judge proceeded to deliver the sentencing. "On the first count, it will be 30 years with 23 years suspended," he pronounced. "On count 2, it will be 10 years with 5 years suspended," the gravity of the situation hung in the air, each word carrying the weight of the impending judgment. Anticipation gripped me as I awaited the determination of whether the sentences would run concurrently or consecutively.

In a moment of relief, the judge declared, "The sentences will run concurrently."

A wave of gratitude washed over me, knowing that the sentences would be served simultaneously. It was a moment of solace amidst the storm. However, despite my gratitude, my thoughts turned to Deanna's mother. She had not been present to hear Deanna's statement or the judge's decision in Deanna's sentencing. Once again, she was absent in Deanna's time of crisis. She had failed her daughter again.

As the judge delivered his verdict, the courtroom held its breath, every eye fixed on Deanna as she absorbed the weight of his decision. Feeling bittersweet, we watched her retreat to the back after waving us goodbye. However, there was one notable absence during that poignant farewell - Deanna's mother, barred from returning after her disruptive outburst. As we gathered our belongings to depart, I helped my mother up from her seat.

As we made our way out of the courtroom, Deanna's attorney joined us. In a hushed exchange, I sought clarification on Deanna's sentence, my heart still racing in my chest. "So that means Deanna would only need to serve 3 and a half years to be eligible for parole, right?" I whispered anxiously.

His confirmation brought a surge of relief. Yes, it was a victory for Deanna, a small reprieve in the face of overwhelming circumstances. And though the prospect of her confinement weighed heavily on my heart, I couldn't help but feel a sense of gratitude for the leniency shown by the judge. It was a delicate balance, a precarious dance between justice and mercy. And while the road ahead would be fraught with challenges, I left that courtroom with a newfound sense of hope, a belief that perhaps, within the shadows, there was still light to be found.

CHAPTER SIX
Statute of Limitations - Child Molestation

After the court trial, I finally felt a bittersweet relief wash over me. My daughter had made a grave mistake, and she was being punished for it. However, at the same time, her heart had always been in the right place, and her intentions were being considered. For that, I was grateful. The judge had acknowledged her thoughts and emotions and shown her a sliver of compassion beneath the weight of the law. Still, the reality of confinement slammed into me like a physical blow. Talking to her then, amidst the shuffling crowd and hushed murmurs, was impossible as she was escorted to the back, so I impatiently waited to talk to her the next day.

As I was leaving the courthouse that day, I stepped outside to fetch something for my mom. When I returned, I saw her engaged in conversation with Mia's ex-boyfriend's grandmother. I quickly made my way over to them and said, "Thank you so much for the kindness you showed Deanna in the courtroom."

She humbly replied, "I was just telling the truth of what I felt." At that moment, I felt overwhelmed with gratitude and continued thanking her on Deanna's behalf.

After meeting the young man's grandmother, I thought to myself, "She's a very nice lady." Honestly, it was surprising how her grandkid could turn out to be so violent. However, I remained polite and thanked her once more for the kind words she had spoken. I couldn't help but think that Deanna's decision not to file assault charges against her grandson may have influenced the grandmother's remarks.

Deanna had the option to press charges, and it could have resulted in him being sent back to jail. Later, Mia informed me that this young man was a convicted felon on probation. As parents, we can't pick our kids' companions, and sometimes, their choices disappoint us. I'm sure Mia's ex-boyfriend's grandmother could resonate with these feelings.

Figure 8: Deanna's Paternal Grandmother and Mia's Ex-boyfriend's Grandmother

Throughout this ordeal with Deanna, I had heard several disturbing things about Mia's ex-boyfriend's character. I didn't particularly like what I learned, and I honestly didn't care if I ever met him. The grandmother's parting words to me were, "I know my grandson can be a handful." I understood the meaning behind her statement and chose not to comment further. I was simply grateful for her kind and compassionate words on Deanna's behalf.

After the open plea hearing, I decided to capture a moment by taking a picture of Deanna's grandmother (my mother) and the grandmother of Mia's ex-boyfriend, who had just spoken heartfelt words on Deanna's behalf.

As I walked out of the courthouse, I noticed Deanna's attorney standing next to her mom's car. Instead of approaching the car, I assumed that the attorney was informing her about the court's decision. It made me reflect on how Deanna's mom had once again let her down during this crucial time. She hadn't been present for Deanna's heartfelt statement and apology in court, she missed hearing the final sentencing, and she couldn't even say goodbye to Deanna as she left the courtroom to begin her confinement.

Once the attorney left, I mustered the courage to walk over to Deanna's mom's car. I shared with her, "Deanna received what I consider to be some compassion from the court." We exchanged pleasantries and bid each other farewell.

I got into the car and drove my mom back home. On our way, I received a text message from Deanna's mom regarding some items that she had lent me concerning Deanna, which I had unintentionally forgotten to return. We made arrangements to meet at a local bookstore before she headed home. I dropped off my mom at her house and then proceeded to meet Deanna's mom to return the items.

The weight of the court hearing lingered heavily in the air as I met Deanna's mom at the bookstore. We both felt the sting of the sentence Deanna had just received. She spoke first with a hint of longing in her voice, "I really hoped she could come home today."

"That would have been ideal," I agreed, "but considering everything, I think the outcome is fair." Deanna's offense was serious, and I reminded her of that. She nodded, acknowledging the severity and admitting some relief that it wasn't worse.

Curious about her courtroom outburst, I asked, "Why did you do that outburst in the courtroom?"

She replied, "When I saw Deanna with the shackles and handcuffs on, I lost it."

Although I nodded, I couldn't bring myself to accept her explanation. I found this confusing because Deanna had entered the courtroom with the same restraints when she walked right in front of us earlier.

When I mentioned this to her, she said, "That is why I reacted that way. I don't remember when she came into the courtroom." I remained silent, but I couldn't help but wonder if her outburst stemmed from a sense of guilt for not being there to support Deanna during all of those crises in Deanna's life.

As we continued discussing Deanna's sentencing, I started talking more about Deanna's childhood and how the molestation had affected her. Deanna's mom proceeded to say, "It did not happen."

I was on the edge of my patience. I defensively asked, "So you think I am lying about what Deanna said?"

"I..." she started, her voice trailing off. It was clear she wasn't sure what to say, caught between denial and the dawning realization that things weren't so black and white.

My frustration mounted with each passing second. We had been divorced for nearly a quarter of a century and separated for nearly 30 years, yet here we were, back in the familiar territory of blame and deflection. As if sensing my annoyance, she launched into a tirade about our marriage, painting a picture of me as a neglectful husband.

"We both had our faults," I countered, my voice level but firm. "I readily admit I wasn't perfect, but no one can say I wasn't a good father to our girls who loved them dearly," I emphasized that this wasn't about dredging up the past—about assigning blame for a failed relationship. This was about Deanna and the future we were both trying to navigate for her. However, she continued to play the victim and divert attention away from the matter at hand.

Therefore, I took another route with the conversation as well. I posed another question, asking, "Do you believe that the Doctor (Dr. Geraldine Chaney) who spoke with Deanna and the counselor who talked with her were lying?" I reminded her that Dr. Chaney had been Deanna's pediatrician since birth, and she held Dr. Chaney in high regard.

To my shock, Deanna's mom responded with, "What report?"

I stared at her in disbelief. "You've never read the report?"

She admitted, "I never read a report."

I was left speechless, unable to utter a single word. This revelation left me in shock, realizing that over the years, she had chosen to believe that her relative had done nothing wrong. She deliberately avoided reading the reports to maintain her belief that it did not happen. All these years, she had chosen to remain blissfully ignorant just because her relative had been involved.

Furthermore, she had access to the reports from the doctor, counselor, and attorney. It was disheartening to hear her inadequate response and excuse. It became clear to me that having a conversation with someone who hadn't even read the reports related to the topic was futile. It seemed pointless to discuss the matter with her, as she had failed to protect her own daughter to protect her relative. The reports were available, as each attorney involved had copies presented in court. I had read a copy, but she persistently refused to read it.

Consequently, I confronted her with the words, "You cannot put your head in the sand and say something did not happen."

I repeated it, emphasizing that she couldn't disregard the reality of the situation. She remained silent, refusing to engage in the conversation. I then shared a personal experience about encountering her relative—the one who had committed the unforgivable act. I told her how I had struggled to keep my cool as he smirked at me with arrogance.

In response, she again started justifying his behavior, saying that it was only a reaction to how I treated her during our marriage. I was exasperated; I reminded her that she hadn't been faultless in our marriage either. Upon reflection, it became apparent that she was still portraying herself as the victim, neglecting to acknowledge the impact of the child molestation on her daughter. Her focus remained on herself and protecting the perpetrator rather than prioritizing her daughter's well-being.

To this day, I feel enraged as I recall how, during our divorce proceedings, Deanna's mom had made multiple attempts to keep the name of her relative out of the final divorce documents. She had requested this from two different Chancery Court Judges, Judge Patricia Wise and Judge William Singletary, who were overseeing our divorce at different stages. However, both judges had rejected her requests, and her relative's name was ultimately disclosed in our final divorce decree.

I had hoped that by discussing this child molestation situation involving her family member and the devastating impact it had on Deanna's life, Deanna's mom and I could work together to help Deanna, especially as she would be released from confinement in the coming years and would need to reestablish her life in society. I knew that the unaddressed issues from her past would still have a negative effect on her if we didn't try to address them in a formal manner. However, with Deanna's mom still maintaining the same mindset as she had years ago regarding Deanna's childhood trauma, I could see that there would be no support forthcoming from her.

As mentioned earlier, during Deanna's recent open plea hearing, the lawyer who represented her was the same one who had represented Deanna's mom in our divorce. He had been involved in the original hearing of the child molestation charges years ago against one of Deanna's mom's relatives. He also mentioned Deanna's history of molestation to the judge during Deanna's current proceedings. Yet, her mom refused to stand by her side.

I couldn't help but wonder that if Deanna had been believed and supported by her mom back then, she might not be in this situation now, and she could have received the help she needed. I felt immense pain thinking about the ordeal Deanna had endured without the support of her mom and her mom's family. Deanna's mom had continued to live right next door to the relative who had committed the molestation. Just knowing this, I felt so mentally drained. I'm sure it must have taken a toll on Deanna's mental health, and I constantly prayed and hoped that Deanna would remain safe.

If only we had handled the situation more proactively when Deanna's doctor had called Deanna's mom for a conference before reporting the incident. Years ago, when Deanna's mom brought some of her family members to the conference at the pediatrician's office, the focus shifted to directing anger at me rather than addressing the situation at hand. Although I never indicated that I wanted any legal action taken against Deanna's mom's relative, Deanna's mom's family remained hostile. My only concern was to protect Deanna. I couldn't understand why we couldn't work together to help Deanna back then. Now, years later, the consequences of Deanna living in an environment where she was not believed and was seen as the problem has become evident. Not once, to my knowledge, did Deanna's mom or her family hold the perpetrator accountable for the harm caused.

In many ways, I found myself navigating a delicate balance between family loyalty and justice when it came to Deanna's situation. Deep down, I harbored a genuine desire to shield her from the harsh glare of the legal system, to spare her the potential trauma of court proceedings and the public exposure of her past. Instead, I hoped we could resolve matters within the confines of our family, away from prying eyes. But our plan to meet at Deanna's doctor's office didn't work out. When we gathered there, it was her mom and the family members who behaved unreasonably. The weight of responsibility for what followed—both the impact on Deanna and the disclosure of her mother's relative's heinous deeds—fell squarely on her mom and those family members present.

As a victim of child molestation, Deanna had already endured immeasurable suffering in her young life. When I broached the subject of writing a book about her experiences, her mom's reaction was predictable. She urged me to bury the past. She fretted over the potential repercussions of dredging up painful memories. But in doing so, she overlooked the fundamental need to protect her own daughter. I reassured her that I wouldn't divulge any details from the book to her, yet I knew that she was once again trying to protect her relative. When she argued, I explained to her that Deanna would have to find ways to cope with this trauma, even after her release from confinement. I also pointed out that her relative's name was clearly stated in the "Bench Report of the Judge" as the perpetrator of the child molestation. It bewildered me why I should feel compelled to shield someone who had never shown remorse for their actions—someone who had moved on with their life while leaving a trail of shattered innocence in their wake. For Deanna's sake and her rights, I knew that the perpetrator had to be brought to light.

For me, it was heartbreaking to face the harsh reality: the one responsible for Deanna's suffering walked freely while she remained trapped in the aftermath of his cruelty. It was a bitter pill to swallow, made even more bitter by her mother's apparent reluctance to acknowledge Deanna's pain. Instead, she seemed content to keep the family blissfully unaware, choosing to bury Deanna's struggles beneath a facade of normalcy.

One day, I gingerly broached the subject, wondering if Deanna's mom had ever considered therapy or counseling for herself over the years; she admitted she hadn't. I suggested that seeking some form of counseling might be beneficial, as we all need someone to talk to at times. Encouragingly, her mother entertained the idea of seeking counseling, albeit with a tentative "maybe." With our conversation drawing to a close, we exchanged pleasantries and farewells. Yet, as I left, a nagging thought lingered: would she ever even read the reports detailing Deanna's ordeal?

I could empathize with the difficulty of confronting such painful truths, especially for a parent. But to willfully ignore the gravity of what had transpired seemed unfathomable. The heart-wrenching memory of my little daughter recounting her ordeal echoed in my mind. Naturally, her mother opted to stay in denial. But in my eyes, there was no justification for her negligence. Reading those reports wasn't just a matter of duty; it was a crucial step toward understanding and supporting her daughter. Instead, it appeared she relied solely on the predator's twisted version of events, a revelation that left me disheartened.

I firmly believe that a parent has no right to disbelieve the incident surrounding their own daughter when they haven't read the report. The worst situation for a parent is to hear their young daughter recount an inappropriate incident. It tears you apart when you feel helpless in protecting her during her time of need. In my opinion, there's no excuse for Deanna's mom not reading the reports. To truly help Deanna, her mom should have read the report. Deanna's mom did not have the right to support the predator at the expense of her own daughter. I find solace in the belief that those who think that they have gotten away with deceitful acts against the vulnerable will eventually be exposed.

The next day, I finally got to talk to my daughter. After a long while, she seemed quite steady. She was no longer tormented by the uncertainty of her future.

"I'm okay, Dad," she reassured me with a quiet strength. "At least I know how long I'll have to serve."

Hearing her calm voice, relief surged through me. We talked, not about the suffocating weight of the past, but about the future that stretched before her, uncertain but full of possibility. "The past," I reminded her gently, "holds valuable lessons." These experiences shape the person we become. I pointed out to her that the sentence could have been much harsher.

Then, Deanna spoke with a hint of something new—hope—in her voice. "Yeah, you're right," she said. "The judge showed some compassion for me when he imposed the sentence."

A flicker of shared belief sparked between us. It was a tiny flame illuminating the path ahead. It wouldn't be easy, but with that shared understanding, the weight of mercy offered a chance for a brighter tomorrow.

It's truly disheartening to witness the lack of consideration from Deanna's mother, especially when strangers like Mia's ex-boyfriend's grandmother are more empathetic toward Deanna's situation. Despite Deanna's involvement in a crime against Mia's ex-boyfriend, his grandmother displayed remarkable support during a conversation we had roughly a month after Deanna's sentencing trial.

Once again, I expressed my deep gratitude for her supportive comments about Deanna during the trial on December 5th, to which she responded with unwavering sincerity, reaffirming that her words were rooted in genuine feelings and truth. Having a background in social work, she had witnessed such cases before. From her experienced perspective, she provided insights into Deanna's resilience and accomplishments in life. She noted that despite the hardships Deanna had faced, she had emerged as a survivor. Furthermore, she emphasized that child molestation transcends racial and ethnic boundaries, a reality she had observed firsthand. Despite the weight of her observations, she maintained a firm belief that the perpetrator owed Deanna an apology for the trauma inflicted upon her during her childhood. She even went on to say that as Deanna's dad, I had the right to request that the perpetrator apologize to Deanna. I did, on one occasion a few years ago, cross paths with the perpetrator and exchanged greetings. At that time, I was trying to bury in my mind the past and had no idea of how Deanna was suffering in life from the events of those childhood traumas. Grateful for her understanding and support, I confided in her about my intention to write a book about Deanna's story, and she encouraged me wholeheartedly. However, she was a little concerned about the exposure of Deanna's past childhood traumas and how it might affect Deanna. I told her that my mom (Deanna's paternal grandmother) had also raised that concern. Our conversation concluded with warm exchanges and heartfelt goodbyes. Since that conversation, I talked with my mom about these concerns, and my mom said that after giving this thought some deep consideration, she thought that it would be best to disclose the complete background of Deanna's mental health concerns. During the process of writing the book, I came across laws that provide child molestation victims with opportunities to seek justice years later. These laws, known by various names in different states, address the statute of limitations for survivors of childhood sexual abuse pursuing civil action against their abusers. Of particular significance are recent legislative reforms in many states that eliminate the statute of limitations entirely for civil cases concerning survivors of childhood sexual abuse. This allows survivors to come forward at any time to seek compensation for the abuse they suffered, regardless of how much time has passed. It's a significant step towards justice and healing for survivors like Deanna.

As I delved into the complexities of seeking justice for survivors of childhood sexual abuse, one aspect weighed heavily on my mind: the role of guardians in protecting innocent children from harm. In my view, significant emphasis should be placed on the role of guardians, as they are the figures to whom innocent children look for protection. It is the responsibility of the guardian to establish appropriate parameters to safeguard the child. If the guardian fails to implement the necessary measures, they should be held accountable alongside the perpetrator of the abuse.

My exploration into the research on child traumas has revealed the profound and enduring impact of child sexual abuse, which is determined by the severity and frequency of the traumas experienced. Individuals who have endured multiple traumas akin to Deanna's experiences and received limited parental support are at risk of developing post-traumatic stress disorder, depression, and anxiety. It is disheartening to acknowledge that the adults and systems in place to protect my daughter failed to do so.

In 2019, California enacted the California Child Victims Act, which came into effect in January 2020, extending the statute of limitations for survivors of childhood sexual abuse to pursue civil action against their abusers. This Act extends the time limit to the later of twenty-two years after the minor's 18th birthday or within five years of the date the victim discovered a psychological injury resulting from the childhood sexual assault in their adulthood. For those who have experienced sexual abuse in California, I encourage reaching out to Helping Survivors for comprehensive guidance on rights and options to facilitate informed decisions in their healing journey.

Under the California Child Victims Act, justice is made more attainable for many survivors of sexual abuse, as the legal definition of childhood sexual abuse has been broadened to include sexual assault. This expansion allows for more offenses against minors to be actionable, offering a sense of closure to a greater number of abuse victims.

In 2020, House Bill 492 was unanimously passed in the Louisiana Senate, entirely removing the statute of limitations on civil cases. This significant development empowers survivors to come forward at any time to seek compensation for childhood sexual abuse, irrespective of the time that has elapsed.

In Mississippi, there exists no criminal statute of limitations for numerous child sexual abuse felonies, such as rape, felonious abuse or battery of a child, and other related offenses. The statute of limitations for sexual battery or fondling of a vulnerable person is set at 5 years from the offense.

A number of states have entirely removed the criminal statutes of limitations for child sexual abuse cases, including Arizona, Arkansas, California, Colorado, Florida, Georgia, Hawaii, Idaho, Indiana, Kansas, Kentucky, Louisiana, Maine, Michigan, Minnesota, Mississippi, New Jersey, New Mexico, New York, North Carolina, Pennsylvania, Rhode Island, South Dakota, Texas, Utah, Vermont, Virginia, Washington, West Virginia, and Wisconsin. Moreover, Alabama, Arkansas, Minnesota, Nebraska, and Tennessee have taken the extra step of terminating the statutes of limitations for both felony child sexual abuse cases and some misdemeanors.

States such as Connecticut, Delaware, Illinois, Iowa, Maryland, Missouri, Montana, South Carolina, and Wyoming allow unlimited time to file criminal charges for any molestation crime, irrespective of whether it's charged as a felony or a misdemeanor. As of now, only Massachusetts, Nevada, New Hampshire, North Dakota, Ohio, Oklahoma, and Oregon still have a statute of limitations in criminal sexual assault cases involving minors.

As I navigated the legal intricacies, I realized the importance of empowering survivors with knowledge about their rights and options. I encouraged individuals to reach out to their attorney general's office or local legislators to learn more about the statutes of limitations for child sexual abuse in their respective states.

As I reflect on the societal response to the horrors of such monstrous crimes, I see a glimmer of hope. Finally, our society is beginning to condemn these sins and stand up for justice. This is great progress in allowing those who have suffered from some of these unspeakable acts to have their day in court at a later date, holding those who are accountable for their actions. On the other hand, we need to be more compassionate for those who have made a wrong decision because of the effects of their varied traumas. Yet, amidst this progress, I cannot help but notice a troubling pattern of hypocrisy that pervades our communities. It strikes me how, when celebrities make mistakes or poor decisions, there often seems to be a more forgiving attitude. Society is quick to extend second chances and offer the benefit of the doubt. However, when it comes to ordinary individuals, the same level of empathy and understanding is often lacking. Mistakes are harshly judged, and opportunities for redemption are scarce. What's more, celebrities possess a multitude of platforms to express their thoughts and clarify misunderstandings. Whether through television interviews, talk shows, or the unwavering support of media spokespersons, they have ample opportunities to set the record straight. In contrast, individuals like Deanna are denied such platforms and opportunities for self-expression.

It is this disparity in treatment that fuels my determination to support Deanna by sharing the details of her life events in this book. Through this medium, I aim to provide her with a voice, to shed light on her experiences, and to advocate for the justice and empathy that every individual, regardless of their status, deserves. It is my hope that by amplifying her story, we can inspire greater understanding, compassion, and solidarity within our society.

Throughout my life, I've always maintained that I'm not overly concerned with what others think of me. And to this day, that remains true. However, when it comes to my daughters, particularly Deanna, I find myself deeply concerned about how society perceives them. I've pondered extensively on how I want society to view Deanna. Did I want her to be seen as a societal outcast, a felon with a reckless disregard for life and the law? Or did I want society to understand the profound struggles she faced with her mental health, exacerbated by the lack of support from those tasked with protecting her? It weighed heavily on my mind that those who inflicted childhood traumas upon her received more respect and support than she ever did.

It was this internal debate that ultimately led me to the decision to write this book - to expose those who played a significant role in harming Deanna's mental health. I knew that by sharing her story, I could shed light on the injustices she faced and advocate for greater understanding and empathy toward individuals struggling with similar challenges. Therefore, I approached Deanna with the idea of writing a book about her story, and her response filled me with gratitude. She was genuinely touched and thankful that I would take the time to tell her story. However, I made sure to explain to her that in order to paint a complete picture of her life, some sensitive information would need to be disclosed. Deanna understood the necessity of revealing certain personal and sensitive details to accurately convey her experiences, particularly those related to her confinement. With her blessing and understanding, I picked up my pen to share her story and reflected on the kind soul of my daughter.

CHAPTER SEVEN
The Journey of Healing

Healing is rarely a comfortable journey. The path often demands we confront unpleasant truths about ourselves, past experiences, or the world around us. These truths can be painful, forcing us to grapple with past hurts or accept uncomfortable realities. However, by avoiding these truths, we risk building our healing on a foundation of sand. Only by acknowledging the entirety of our situation can we begin to build genuine resilience and move forward with authenticity. Unfortunately, we didn't realize this earlier.

My deepest regret is that for so long, Deanna has been hurting from past experiences, bleeding inside with unspoken pain. We, as a family, never addressed it. It was like we were afraid to even touch the fire, even though the flames were already burning her. Now, I understand that this silence hasn't helped. Deanna needs to confront what happened: the good, the bad, and the ugly.

That's why I want Deanna to read these words. I want them to be a part of her journey, a guidepost on the road to recovery from all the ordeals she's faced. Because here's the truth: if we, as a family, had faced those issues head-on years ago, if we'd talked about them openly instead of hiding them in the shadows, maybe that dreadful day on August 21st, 2021, wouldn't have happened. It may feel like pretending everything's fine, like sweeping the hurt under the rug, will somehow make it disappear. However, ignoring the issues will only make them escalate.

After that day, Deanna's mom informed me that she knew about all of Deanna's mental health issues. These problems were mentioned in a report from Deanna's counselors, which I read a few days before her trial. Surprisingly, I had no knowledge of Deanna's mental health challenges back then. However, the same could not be said about her mother. It's quite astonishing how she could turn a blind eye to her daughter's suffering. Had those mental health concerns been addressed when they were first discovered, Deanna wouldn't be in her current situation today. It's important to remember that when we want to assist our family members with certain problems, we can't simply ignore them and hope they'll disappear. Keeping things hidden doesn't bring any benefit to the individual in need.

Through the process of writing this book, I've gained valuable insights into the journey of healing. It has also taught me that I possess the strength to support my daughter. This strength lies in my ability to discuss her challenges without getting overwhelmed by emotions. Those who assist her in healing must remain resilient when faced with these delicate matters. Though it can be tough, writing this book has been a source of healing for me as well. I hadn't realized, as Deanna's father, that I needed to heal from the childhood traumas she endured.

As I navigate through this journey of healing, I want to pose some questions to illuminate the path of recovery from childhood trauma. Stated below are the questions:

Can Childhood Trauma Ever Be Healed?

Healing from childhood trauma is a challenging journey that can span many years and, for some, even a lifetime. However, it is indeed possible to overcome these experiences. In order to heal from childhood trauma, it is crucial to address and complete the recovery process that should have taken place long ago when the traumatic incident occurred. When utilizing these helpful suggestions and activities, it may be beneficial to start with a less severe traumatic experience before gradually progressing towards more significant traumas. This allows for mastering the techniques and applying them to more difficult situations, fostering healing along the way.

How Long Does It Take to Heal from Childhood Trauma?

Healing from childhood trauma is a unique journey for each person. It depends greatly on the individual and the nature of their traumatic experiences. For some, healing might take a long time, especially if the trauma is severe. For others, it might take as little as six months to a year. The duration also depends on the type of treatment chosen. It can take time to find the right therapy or combination of therapies, such as medication and counseling, that work best for the healing process.

The people we surround ourselves with play a significant role in our healing journey. We are greatly influenced by those around us, especially family members, because we trust and love them. Often, we put a lot of weight on their opinions. However, during the healing process, it's crucial to be around people who believe in us and encourage us. Positive influences are vital, as healing can be a delicate time with emotions running high. We need support to build our self-belief. It's also important not to blame ourselves while healing. Self-blame can be very harmful and can hinder our progress. We need to be kind to ourselves and understand that healing takes time and patience. It's a fragile period, and having a positive, supportive environment can make a big difference in our recovery.

One of the most important aspects of healing is TIME. We often hear that healing takes time, and I couldn't agree more. However, it can be a very difficult and long process if we don't understand how to navigate this concept of time. This should be approached one step at a time, much like setting and achieving goals. When helping someone set goals, they should be realistic and attainable. They shouldn't be out of reach. Goals should be something we can work towards, with many smaller achievements along the way toward the ultimate goal of recovery, no matter what challenges we face in life.

Helping someone to heal also involves understanding that we all have a purpose in life. We shouldn't run from it or be ashamed of it. Instead, we should embrace it and realize that we have the ability to make those around us feel better. We can learn from our mistakes and teach others from our experiences. This understanding helps us to move forward and grow stronger through the healing process.

The memorable words of the esteemed orator Martin Luther King, Jr. have always resonated with me. "If I can help somebody as I pass along if I can cheer somebody with a word or a song, and if I can show somebody he's traveling wrong, then my living will not be in vain."

I've taken his words to heart, and I want to inspire the same values in my daughter.

Today, I've come to a realization that Deanna's journey toward healing hinges on a crucial first step - her mother's unwavering empathy. Deanna needs her mother to truly understand the depth of her struggles. This understanding can manifest in two ways: firm belief in Deanna's story or, if that's not possible, creating space through a temporary separation. While the latter option may be a difficult truth to face, it's important to acknowledge that a supportive environment is paramount for healing. There's no doubt that Deanna cherishes her mother and craves her support. However, for Deanna to embark on this healing journey, there needs to be a sense of accountability from those closest to her, especially her mother. Their role goes beyond simply being present; it involves actively fostering an environment that empowers Deanna's recovery. I believe the following transformations in her life would promote her healing:

1. The process of healing for Deanna begins with her mother expressing remorse and offering an apology for not providing the support and belief she needed.

2. The relatives of Deanna's mother should take responsibility and apologize to Deanna for the traumatic experiences that she endured during her early childhood.

3. The administrators at Madison County School should issue an apology to Deanna for their mishandling of the reported childhood trauma situation during her time in high school.

During Deanna's court hearing, I tried to play my part as her father. Although I couldn't help her earlier, I openly acknowledged my shortcomings and apologized for not seeking the necessary counseling to address the effects of her childhood traumas.

This is definitely a start for Deanna as she moves forward with her healing process.

I believe in so many ways, our lives are running like a business. In a book that I wrote in 2009, titled; "The Ultimate Business Bible," I talked about removing certain people from your life who may not have your best interest at heart. In the book, I referred to such people as CAVE people (Citizen Against Virtually Everything). The following is what I wrote about Cave People in that book:

"If our dreams are always torn down and shattered by that same person over and over again, that person may be the CAVE person in your life. As difficult as you might want to think, that cave person could be your spouse, your best friend, a close relative, or, sad to say, even your parents. It is very difficult to move forward with great business aspirations when someone keeps telling you that you can't. Successful people surround themselves with other successful people. I am a believer that people feed off of each other. You have to admit that we react to the ideas of those who we care about the most. A lot of thought should go into determining who those "CAVE" people are in your life and remove them."

This is my message to Deanna. It's true that certain individuals in your life, whom we may refer to as CAVE people, can hold you back from healing and living a healthy life. If these people genuinely loved and cared for you, they wouldn't be acting as CAVE people in your life. I understand that it can be incredibly difficult to process this decision, especially considering who some of these individuals may be. However, if you truly want to live a healthier life, it's important to confront the fact that you may need to remove these people from your life. Realizing that what you thought you had and what you actually have are not the same. It's important to focus on your own well-being and prioritize your healing process. Sometimes, letting go of those who don't believe in you is necessary for your personal growth and happiness.

By removing the negative influences from your life, you can create a more positive environment for yourself where you can thrive and lead a healthier life.

Deanna and I have regular conversations while she is in confinement, where I update her on how everyone in the family is doing, and she fills me in on her situation there. One particular phone call stands out in my memory, which took place on April 6, 2024. During the call, we exchanged greetings and pleasantries. At one point, Deanna expressed her deep appreciation for her parents. She also mentioned how grateful she felt to have a place to come to once she was released from confinement. She shared that there are individuals in the facility who have no destination to go to upon their release, leaving them uncertain and worried. In response, I assured her that she will always have a place to call home and that our love for her is unwavering.

During one of our conversations, I shared an analogy with Deanna that resonated with her deeply. I explained to her that in life, each of us is dealt a handful of cards to navigate through our journey. I emphasized that we often don't know what cards we have until they are given to us. Some of these cards may be positive and beneficial, while others may be challenging or difficult to handle. Nevertheless, we have no choice but to play the hand that we are dealt with.

Deanna expressed her gratitude for the analogy and told me that it made a lot of sense to her. She found comfort in the idea and assured me that she would hold onto it. It seemed to offer her a perspective and understanding that resonated with her own experiences.

This exchange with Deanna reminded me of a conversation that I had with her a few years ago. During that conversation, Deanna mentioned that her mom had been quite concerned about the family matters concerning Deanna's abuser. She was even more emotionally invested in those matters than she had ever been in her daughter's trauma. Deanna said that her mom's main priority in life was to make sure that Deanna's abusers' family concerns were taken care of, and it made her feel a loss of closeness to her mom because of where her mom's priorities were at the time. This brought back thoughts of that conversation a few years ago when I had to really control my sadness because Deanna and I had never discussed her childhood traumas during her adult life, and I was feeling her pain at that time. I was upset internally, and I was trying not to show my emotions to Deanna. I could really feel her hurt during the conversation that we had a few years ago. My thoughts regarding Deanna's mom at that point were that she just did not care, or she had no idea of the pain that she was inflicting on Deanna. I was so helpless and lost at that time. I didn't know how to help Deanna. I used the only thing I could use – prayer.

During our conversation, I informed Deanna about a letter that was sent to her at the facility but ended up being returned to my mom's (Deanna's grandmother) house. I explained that the letter was from her mom, and her mom had used granny's return address on the envelope. Curious about the reason behind this, I asked Deanna why she thought her mom had chosen to do so.

Deanna shared her belief that her mom didn't want the letter to be returned to her own address in case it didn't reach Deanna. I was taken aback and asked her why her mom would not want anyone to know where she was. Deanna explained that her mom tells anyone who inquires about her whereabouts that she is simply out of town.

Furthermore, Deanna mentioned that whenever she talks on the phone with her mom, and someone is around, her mom speaks in a low voice.

During their conversation, Deanna revealed that when she speaks to her mom at her grandparents' (Deanna's maternal grandparents) house, her mom intentionally leaves the room where her grandparents are present. Deanna interpreted this behavior as her mom not wanting her grandparents to know that she was talking to Deanna on the phone. She recounted a recent incident where her mom left the room because some of her mom's sisters were present. Deanna expressed her concerns to her mom, telling her that she was being excessively secretive.

In response, I reassured Deanna that given the widespread media coverage of her ordeal on TV and the internet, it is likely that most people already know about her situation. I then posed a question to Deanna, asking if she thought her mom was ashamed of her and her circumstances. Deanna responded with a heartfelt "Yes." This revelation deeply saddened me, and I made sure to express my unwavering support and love for Deanna. I assured her that I was not ashamed of her or anything that she had gone through in life and that I would always be there to support her in any way she needed. Deanna thanked me and reciprocated the love.

During that same conversation, Deanna also mentioned that her mom casually mentioned the name of the relative who had been the abuser during her childhood trauma. Deanna found her mom's mention of the relative to be cavalier and lacking sensitivity.

It's important for people to understand that survivors of child abuse don't want to hear their abuser's name mentioned in a positive way, especially from someone they love. This can cause more emotional pain and can be a form of ongoing abuse. It's not healthy to impose our own thoughts or beliefs onto someone else's trauma.

To heal from childhood trauma, survivors need to go through a healing process that should have started when the abuse happened. This involves acknowledging the impact of the trauma, respecting the survivor's coping mechanisms, and providing a safe space for them to talk about their experiences and seek support.

Supporting a survivor of abuse means creating a safe and understanding environment, allowing them to open up at their own pace, and respecting their boundaries. It's crucial to show empathy, validation, and unconditional love, letting them know that they're not alone and their experiences are valid. Professional help, like therapy, can also be beneficial in the healing process.

Healing from childhood trauma is a unique and complex journey, and it's important to approach it with sensitivity, compassion, and a willingness to learn and support.

It's worth noting that survivors in their adult healing process choose to still have relationships with their abusers, even though they hate the abuse. This can be complicated, especially when the abuser is a family member or close friend. It's important to respect the survivor's choices and offer support without judgment.

In this book, I not only aim to share my daughter's story but also aim to educate people about trauma. After all, acceptance is the first step towards recovery.

Accepting That You Have Childhood Trauma

Coming to terms with childhood trauma can be a difficult and painful process. However, it is essential to acknowledge these experiences in order to begin the healing journey. Denying or minimizing the impact of the trauma can lead to internalized pain and unresolved emotions. Over time, these suppressed feelings may manifest as self-blame, shame, or guilt. It is important to recognize that the trauma did occur and that you are not at fault. By acknowledging and accepting your childhood trauma, you can regain a sense of control and take steps toward healing.

Distancing Yourself from Traumatic Events

When addressing childhood trauma, it's crucial to understand that the process of healing is gradual and requires persistence and support. One technique that may be helpful on this journey is adopting a self-reflective stance. This involves observing oneself from a detached perspective to minimize emotional reactions when examining past experiences.

Research has indicated that taking a self-reflective stance can yield positive outcomes for individuals who have experienced post-traumatic stress disorder. It can result in a reduction of intense emotional and physical responses triggered by traumatic events. Rather than avoiding or suppressing emotions, it is important to develop a sense of inner stability and self-empowerment, allowing for a healthy distance between oneself and distressing memories or feelings.

It might seem like a long time until my daughter walks out of the prison. Perhaps it would take her years or even decades to completely heal. However, whenever she is free, I want to guide her throughout her journey every step of the way. I'm no professional, but I try my best to make up for all those years. I couldn't support her, and this book is my attempt. Below, I've listed a few ways to heal childhood trauma in hopes that Deanna would find something that would facilitate her healing:

Ways to Heal Your Childhood Trauma

1. Acknowledge the Trauma: The first step in healing is to recognize and accept the trauma for what it is. Many childhood trauma survivors spend years downplaying the event or pretending it didn't happen, often burdened by feelings of guilt or self-blame. To start healing, it's crucial to acknowledge that a traumatic event did occur and understand that it was not your fault. This acceptance is the foundation for moving forward.

2. Reclaim Your Power: Feelings of helplessness from childhood can linger into adulthood, making you feel like a victim, leading to choices driven by past pain. When you feel like a victim, your past controls your present. But once you start to overcome your pain, you gain control over your present. It's not easy, and the struggle between past and present may continue, but by letting go of the old defenses and coping mechanisms from your childhood, you can start to reclaim your life and heal.

3. Seek Support and Stay Connected: It's natural for trauma survivors to want to withdraw from others, but isolation only makes things worse. A significant part of healing is connecting with people. Make an effort to maintain your relationships and seek support. Talk to a trusted family member, friend, or counselor, and consider joining a support group for childhood trauma survivors. These connections can provide much-needed emotional support.

4. Prioritize Your Health: Being physically healthy can improve your ability to cope with stress. Establish a daily routine that includes plenty of rest, a balanced diet, and regular exercise. Avoid alcohol and drugs, as they might offer temporary relief but will eventually increase feelings of depression, anxiety, and isolation, worsening your trauma

symptoms. Taking care of your body helps create a stable foundation for emotional healing.

5. Learn Acceptance and Letting Go: Acceptance doesn't mean that you're embracing or agreeing with your trauma. It means deciding how to handle it. You can choose to let it dominate your life, or you can choose to let it go. Letting go isn't an instant fix; it means not letting bad memories and feelings from a difficult childhood prevent you from living a fulfilling life now. It's about deciding to move forward despite the past.

6. Replace Bad Habits with Positive Ones: Bad habits, whether it's negativity, mistrust, or turning to substances for relief, can be hard to break. These habits are often used to avoid reliving the pain and trauma of childhood. A therapist or support group can provide tools to help you break these bad habits and develop healthier ones. Positive habits can lead to better coping mechanisms and a more balanced life.

7. Be Patient with Yourself: Healing from childhood trauma is a long process. When deeply hurt as a child, you develop strong emotions, defense mechanisms, and distorted perceptions that are hard to let go of. It takes time and effort to release these feelings. Be patient and honor your progress, no matter how small it may seem. Celebrate the little victories as they contribute to the overall journey of healing. Remember, you were not responsible for the trauma you experienced, and like any wound, trauma requires time and proper care to heal.

8. Get Support: Many trauma survivors feel the urge to isolate themselves, but resisting this urge is crucial. Healing is much easier when you maintain relationships and seek continuous support from friends, family, romantic partners, support groups, and mental health

professionals. These connections can offer encouragement and a sense of belonging, making the healing process more manageable.

Healing childhood trauma is never easy, but it can become more manageable with the support of others. The right treatment can transform your life, even after years of trauma. By working with a mental health professional and relying on your support network, you can start your journey toward healing. With time, patience, and continuous effort, you can overcome the trauma and become the best version of yourself.

My narrative isn't just for my daughter, Deanna, but also for everyone who loves her and wants to support her in this journey.

Ways to Support a Loved One Who Experienced Childhood Abuse

Childhood abuse leaves deep scars that can affect a person's mental and emotional health for a long time. Helping a friend or loved one who experienced abuse as a child can play a crucial role in their recovery.

Understanding the Impact of Childhood Abuse

Childhood abuse can cause physical, emotional, and psychological harm. It often leads to feelings of shame, guilt, and self-blame, which can damage a person's self-esteem and self-image. It can also create trust issues, making it hard to form healthy relationships. By understanding these impacts, you can offer the necessary support and validation.

1. Listen: One of the most valuable things you can do is to listen without judgment. Let them share their story at their own pace.

Acknowledge their feelings and experiences, and never interrupt or minimize what they're saying. Validate their emotions and reassure them that the abuse was not their fault and they deserve support and love.

2. Believe and Support: Often, accounts of childhood abuse are met with skepticism, which can worsen the trauma. It's crucial to let survivors know that you believe them. Accept their story without question and avoid suggesting what they could have done differently.

3. Create a Safe and Supportive Environment: Providing a safe, supportive, and non-judgmental environment is key to their healing. Make them feel comfortable sharing their experiences and emotions at their own pace. Encourage them to take their time and share as much or as little as they want.

4. Connect Them with Resources: There are many resources available for those who have experienced childhood abuse, such as therapy and support groups. Encourage your loved one to seek out these resources and offer to help them find the right support. Point them to hotlines and websites that offer assistance and information.

5. Respect Their Boundaries and Decisions: Respecting your loved one's boundaries and decisions is crucial. Healing from childhood abuse is a long process, and patience is essential. Support them and offer encouragement, but let them decide how to share their story and what steps to take next. This respect will empower them on their healing journey.

6. Educate Yourself on the Impact of Childhood Abuse: If you haven't experienced childhood abuse, it can be hard to grasp its full impact. Educate yourself about the different types and effects of

childhood abuse to better understand the challenges your loved one faces.

7. Take Care of Yourself: Supporting someone who has experienced childhood abuse can be emotionally draining. Make sure to take care of your own emotional well-being and seek support from friends, family, or a support group for caretakers of abuse survivors.

Supporting survivors of childhood abuse is challenging but vital. It requires patience, empathy, and a non-judgmental attitude. Your love and support can make a significant difference in their recovery.

A Message for Deanna

Deanna, I want you to know that your journey to healing is not one you have to take alone. We are all here for you, ready to support and walk with you every step of the way. Your strength and resilience inspire us all, and we believe in you wholeheartedly. Remember, you are not defined by your past but by your courage to overcome it. Together, we will navigate this path to healing, and I am confident that you will emerge stronger and more empowered than ever before. We love you dearly and are here to lift you, always.

hey dad:

How are you, Mia, Lenora, Marissa + granny? It feels strange to write a letter instead of texting, calling or driving over to your house, but life has temporarily changed for me. You've always told me to not trust everybody but to only trust my grandparents, parents + siblings. Because of my loyalty + love for my sister, my attempt at justice sent me to prison. Sometimes we need time to reflect on past actions to make better decisions in the future, so I accept that I'm here. All things happen for a reason and in God's plan, so I'm making the best use of my time. While I'm here, I'm focusing on maintaining a close relationship with God, reaching my goal weight of 200 lbs (I'm currently 260 lbs!), + becoming a better person spiritually, physically, + mentally. Since being in prison for a little over 2 months, I've lost 40 lbs, registered for my first class that starts tomorrow, started working weekdays in the gym, + pray and read my bible daily. I'm learning life skills to take with me when I'm back home. I know when I'm released back into the free world, I will have so much appreciation for life. I once lived a life that just passed by but I didn't live. I just stuck to comfort + routine to determine my days. I will now take advantage of all life has to offer with my new body, new mind, + renewed relationship with Christ. Thankfully, I serve a God who doesn't put more on us than we can bare. I am grateful, thankful + blessed for God's grace. There isn't anything I go through that is too tough to handle. Although I'm physically in prison, my mind will never be imprisoned. There are so many books, movies, investments, businesses, etc that I have to accomplish. While I have this free time, it's only a matter of which to start first.

I love you all + will be home soon.

Remember: This too shall pass.

Figure 9: A letter from Deanna

CHAPTER EIGHT
Understanding Child Molestation

When Deanna told me about the case of her molestation years ago, I often wondered if I had handled it correctly. I didn't have any experience with this, so I just went with my gut. I later learned some tips on how to handle this situation. There were some guidelines from the American Academy of Child Adolescent & Psychiatry (AACAP) on how to handle the position I was in, and I was glad that I did it in a way that they thought was right.

Often, when a kid tells an adult that they have been sexually abused, the adult may feel bad and not know what to say or do. Because of this, I wanted to share some information that I think will help people who may be going through similar things that I did many years ago. As parents or responsible adults, we would never let our kids go through such horrible experiences. In life, we have to deal with tough events that we often don't see coming, and that's a part of life. It is important that we accept such a turn of unfortunate events.

Although these circumstances are extremely distressing, there's always the best course of action that an adult must take. If a child tells you in a general way that they think they have been sexually abused, let them talk about it. Don't say anything negative. Show the child that you hear and understand what they are saying.

Psychologists who work with kids and teens have found that kids who are heard and understood are more likely to share and have fewer mental problems than kids who are ignored or not believed. For a child to heal from the pain of sexual abuse, it's very important that you listen to them without judging them. Tell the kid that sharing is the right thing to do.

If the child is close to the abuser, they might feel bad about telling anyone about it. For example, if the abuser said they would hurt the child or other family members if they told on them, the child might be scared. Tell the child that the sexual abuse did not happen because of them. Most kids will try to make sense of being abused by thinking that they did something wrong or that they are being punished for something they did or didn't do. And finally, offer to protect the child. Tell them that you will act right away to stop the abuse.

It shouldn't just be limited to your words. You have to report any signs that indicate a child is being abused. Child Protection Agency in your area should be told about any abuse that happens in the family. Tell the cops if the abuse happens somewhere other than the family. People who report crimes in good faith are not prosecuted by the law. The organization that gets the report will look into it and do something to keep the child safe.

Parents should talk to their child's pediatrician or family doctor. This doctor may be able to send them to a doctor who specializes in treating and evaluating sexual abuse. The doctor will examine the child and fix any physical problems that may have been caused by the abuse. The doctor will also look for evidence to help protect the child and reassure the child that everything is okay.

Kids who have been sexually abused should be evaluated by a child and adolescent psychiatrist or another qualified mental health professional. This is to find out how the abuse has changed them and to see if they need ongoing professional help to deal with the trauma of the abuse. The therapist for children and teens can also help other family members who may be upset about the abuse.

Most claims that children have been sexually abused are true, but sometimes fake claims are made during custody battles or other times. The court will sometimes ask a child and adolescent psychiatrist to help them figure out if the child is telling the truth or if speaking the truth about the abuse may possibly hurt the child. Certain things, like videotaping, frequent breaks, keeping spectators out, and letting the child choose not to look at the accused, render the experience much less stressful for the kid.

When adults hurt kids, they are always to blame. Children who are abused should never be blamed, even if the abuser says that the child agreed or allowed the abuse. Just because a teen under 18 has told an abuser that he or she agrees doesn't mean that the abuse is ok or doesn't hurt the child. A caring and supportive reaction is the first thing that should happen when a child tells someone about being sexually abused. This will help the child get help and rebuild their trust in adults.

Misunderstandings About How Children Respond to Abuse

A lot of adults think that if a kid had a bad or traumatic emotional, physical, or sexual experience with an adult, the child would tell them. People think nothing happens if the child doesn't say anything. Adults may think that a kid will forget about being abused or exploited if they don't see any bad effects or only notice small ones. Sometimes, this is the case even when the abuse or exploitation is known to have happened. They might really believe that it's *"best not to focus on a bad memory."*

A lot of adults also think that sexual abuse only includes violent rape or major injuries to the body when it comes to children. It's not clear to them that different types of physical and mental abuse can do very bad things. Researchers have found that mental abuse can be worse for the mind than physical abuse. Sexualized interactions with kids, like touching them without permission, showing them pornography, watching them do sexual acts, or even making sexually degrading or frightening comments, can do a lot of damage that lasts for a long time. All of these things happen when adults break their promises to children and abuse their trust. They can all hurt a child's mind, body, relationships, and their ability to do well in school and at work for a long time.

Coping with the Shock of Intrafamilial Sexual Abuse

The term 'intrafamilial sexual abuse' refers to sexual abuse that happens within the family. This kind of abuse happens when a family member performs or lets a child see sexual acts or actions. The "family member" doesn't have to be a blood relative; it could be a close friend, godparent, or someone else who is 'part of the family'.

When you find out that someone you love and trust has sexually abused your child, it can be very stressful and make you feel very shocked, angry, confused, in denial, and guilty. You will need time, strength, and support from your extended family, your community, and professionals in law enforcement, child protection, and mental health services to deal with these responses and help your child recover from the abuse. It might be hard, but you should tell the police if your child tells them about sexual abuse.

It can be hard to face the truth about sexual abuse in the family. But if you tell everyone about it, you can help your family heal and protect your child so that he or she can grow up to be a healthy, happy adult.

The Effect of Intrafamilial Abuse

More than half of all the children who are abused are either sexually abused by a parent or other family member. Because of this, victims of sexual abuse in the family may not tell anyone about it for weeks, months, or even longer, and it may take even longer to tell everyone all the facts. Kids who come from countries that don't like talking about sex or sexuality might be even less likely to say anything.

Children and teens who have been sexually abused by a family member often have a hard time with self-doubt, self-blame, fear of the attacker, and stress over what telling their family about it would lead to. In an effort to make things better in the family, they may change their story or even say that the abuse never happened. It's normal for kids to change their minds or "take back" what they said, which doesn't mean they were lying about being abused.

Children who have been abused by a family member may feel pressured to lie because telling the truth could hurt the family, or there wouldn't be enough help from the family. Your child and your family can deal with what happened better if you talk to a counselor who specializes in child sexual abuse. Counseling can help your child and your family deal with the stress and other effects of being sexually abused. Your child and the rest of the family can get over the abuse and heal with the right help.

When an adult sexually abuses a child, it puts a huge strain on their family bonds. Some family members might not think the abuser could do something like that and pick a side (or feel pressured to pick a side) over who is telling the truth. Family members may also find it hard to balance their love for both the attacker and the victim. Some families may say things like "lock him up and throw away the key" or "hate the sin but love the sinner" when they talk about the abuser. When people in the same family have different ideas about what is loyal, fair, just, forgiving, and responsible, it can cause problems.

For many moms, the hardest part is dealing with how they feel about their child telling them. If your child tells you that they have been sexually abused, how you react can have a big impact on how quickly they recover.

Coping with Your Own Reactions

When you first hear that a family member has sexually abused your child, you might feel shocked, angry, confused, and find it difficult to believe it. If you were sexually abused as a child, the news may make you feel even worse and cause you more confusion.

Take it easy if you have painful doubts about your child, especially if the abuser is someone you love or depend on, like a husband, boyfriend, or grandparent. That person who abused your child will almost certainly say they didn't do it, so you may have to choose which family member is telling the truth and think about what will happen if you believe one over the other. Many parents find it easy to think that their child has been abused when the child is very young.

Parents who have always believed their children may feel guilty that they could not stop the abuse or that they did not notice the signs until the kid told them. It's good to remember that we can't read minds or know what might happen in the future, even though hindsight is 20/20. Many of the "clues" that seem clear now are vague behaviors (like being more irritable, not sleeping well, etc.) that not even a mental health worker could have necessarily seen as signs of the child being sexually abused.

Throughout most of human history, kids who told adults about sexual abuse were rarely believed or helped. When kids told their parents about abuse, they were told to keep quiet or forget about it, and some were even scolded and punished for "telling lies." These kids not only had to deal with the abuse, but they also felt cheated and abandoned by the people who were supposed to protect them.

When you find out that your own child has been mistreated, especially by a family member, it can bring up a lot of painful memories and feelings that you haven't dealt with. This is an important part of being able to help your child: getting help for yourself. With the help of parents who care about and protect them, children who have been sexually abused can get better.

When a child has been abused in the family, the most helpful person they have is a parent who did nothing wrong. Even though it might be hard, telling someone about sexual abuse by a family member is the best thing you can do to help everyone heal.

How do the Effects of Trauma Develop?

It's normal to feel traumatized after being abused. Children who are mistreated might not be able to figure out what exactly might be wrong with them. But their bodies are attuned to identify the signs when they are in danger, and even as adults, those bodies may still remember being abused.

Because of this, many women who have been abused are easily upset by things that make them think of the abuse. They may feel like they are going through the traumatic event again. They may have flashbacks, which are rapid, strong, and unpleasant memories of the horrible times.

There are different ways for women to deal with those painful feelings. For instance, they might get an eating disorder, abuse drugs or alcohol, or hurt themselves. These things might help women deal with their turmoil for a while. But ultimately, such unhealthy behaviors lead to them feeling lonelier. They can aggravate anxiety and sleep problems. Women who have been through trauma, may feel like they have no control or are "going crazy." She could feel mentally numb or wake up feeling panicked all of a sudden. The woman might not be aware that the things that make her think of the abuse are making her act out.

A lot of people don't know that abuse can have effects on their lives years later, and they don't think that the effects of trauma are related to being abused as a child.

Child Sexual Abuse

If a kid is interacting with an adult or another child and is being used for sexual pleasure by the adult or an observer, this is called child sexual abuse. Sexual abuse can include actions that may or may not include touch. People who engage in touching behavior may touch their vagina, penis, breasts, or buttocks, make oral-genital contact, or have sexual relations. People who don't touch a child may engage in voyeurism (looking at a child's naked body), exhibitionism, or showing pornography to the child.

Abusers don't always use physical force. Instead, they may use games, lies, threats, or other forms of pressure to keep kids quiet. To keep the child interested, abusers often use persuasion and manipulation. This type of behavior is called "grooming," and it can include things like buying gifts or setting up fun activities that can make the target even more confused.

Who is sexually abused?

It is possible for kids of all ages, races, and income backgrounds to be sexually abused. Girls and boys of all ages are abused sexually as children. It happens in all kinds of neighborhoods and towns and in all sorts of countries.

How can you tell if a child is being (or has been) sexually abused?

Children who have been sexually abused may act and feel in many ways that are similar to how children who have been through other types of pain act and feel.

These responses include having frequent nightmares or other sleep problems, acting distant or angry, feeling anxious or depressed, not wanting to be alone with certain people, knowing sexual things, speaking or acting in ways that aren't appropriate for their age, and/or acting in ways that are sexual.

When kids are sexually abused, why don't they tell anyone? There are many reasons a kid might not tell someone they've been sexually abused, such as fear of being removed from the home, threats of physical harm to the child or their family, shame, or guilt.

When a child is abused by someone they care about, they may be afraid of getting that person in trouble. Also, kids often think it was their own fault when they were sexually abused, so they might not tell anyone because they don't want to get in trouble. Very young children might not be able to talk about being abused or might not understand that what the abuser subjected them to was wrong, especially if it is turned into a game.

Why Adults Fail to Protect Children

Almost everyone will say that they would report child abuse if they saw it. A lot of people are sure they'd spot cruel behavior if they saw it. A very small number of people think they would let harmful sexual behavior go on even if they were sure it was happening. Still, the sad truth is that millions of kids in this country are abused every year. A lot of them are right to think that someone knows or should know about what's going on, but that doesn't always do much to help them. Some kids tell adults what's going on to get help and safety, but they are often laughed at, denied, blamed, or even punished.

Harmful Stereotypes Regarding Sexual Predators

Today, there are many dangerous stereotypes prevalent about the kind of people who would sexually abuse children. Tragically, this line of thought makes it harder to protect kids. Some of us still act like bad people, like criminals are the only ones who hurt kids, even though we know this to be false. We think it would be easy for us to spot these people and keep kids safe from them.

That's not true; it's much more complex than that. It's hard to see real threats when people believe these common stereotypes, especially what qualifies someone to be good or bad. These seemingly "good people" who put up a good image in society also make it hard for kids to spot who could be dangerous. They struggle to wrap their minds around why someone who is good to others would be sexually or physically hurting them or failing to treat them with respect.

The truth is that even parents who love and care for their kids sometimes hurt them. Kids can get hurt by grandparents who are too nice and fun. Sometimes coaches and teachers, who are kind and loving, sexually abuse kids. Religious leaders who are very powerful sometimes sexually abuse children. Kids can be sexually harmed by older brothers, cousins, kids down the street, and even fun and caring babysitters. In fact, the person who hurts a child sexually, physically, or mentally is almost never one of those really creepy people that everyone already knows about.

It's hard for most of us to hold two different contradicting ideas regarding how people should act at the same time. That's why we often miss the risk even when it's right in front of us. It's hard, or even scary, to believe that "good" people can have "bad" traits and actions, especially when the "good" person is someone we care about or respect. In order to feel better, we often ignore or change the facts to fit our comforting beliefs.

Why Family Members Take Sides in Sexual Abuse?

When someone is sexually abused, family members may side with the abuser instead of the victim. There could be a reason for this. You may have been holding back for a long time to tell someone close to you something. You plan what you're going to say, but when the big day comes, they don't back you up. Some of you might be shocked or let down. A traumatic event happened to you, and now you have to deal with another traumatic event: your loved ones are siding with the person who hurt you. Things like this shouldn't happen, but they do a lot more often than most people think.

Why does this take place? This is probably the most usual reason: people don't want it to be true. We all know someone who has been sexually abused or attacked, but not many of us will say we know someone who does it.

What happens when a family sides with a person who abuses instead of the survivor?

The people in your family might not be able to help you as much as you need. The family could say that the abuse didn't happen. They might say the abuse never happened or that you're remembering things wrong. Cut down on the abuse. They might try to make the abuse seem like a mistake, an accident, or a misunderstanding. You should take the blame. They might say that you're lying or trying to get their attention. They might make it sound like you agreed with or deserved what happened to you.

Take a stand. People might get mad at you or say they'll avoid you if you tell anyone else. How it might sound:

- "Boys will be boys."
- "It wasn't really a big deal."
- "Do not bring this up again."
- "You have no right to say that about them."
- "Leave the past behind and move on."
- "Most likely, they had no idea what they were doing."
- "They've probably changed since then."

How does child trauma affect mental health?

The person who was sexually abused may have trouble with their mental health afterward. About 81% of women and 35% of men who have been sexually abused will have long-term mental health problems, such as post-traumatic stress disorder (PTSD). It can also lead to revictimization if your loved ones don't believe what you're saying. It's normal to feel worried, confused, sad, helpless, seen, and suspicious.

The denial of sexual abuse can wreak havoc on a survivor's mental health.

"First, they went through something so traumatic, and then when they get the guts to talk about it and ask for help, no one believes them." It makes you feel bad about your own worth and can often make you feel bad about yourself for the rest of your life. Being there for someone without judging them is the best gift a family member can give. They need to believe the victim and tell them it's not their fault. Allow them to share information at their own pace and comfort level as they tell their story.

If childhood sexual abuse is not treated, long-term symptoms can go on through adulthood.

These may include:

- PTSD and anxiety.
- Depression and thoughts of suicide.
- Sexual anxiety and disorders, including having too many or unsafe sexual partners.
- Difficulty setting safe limits with others (e.g., saying no to people) and relationship problems.
- Poor body image and low self-esteem.
- Unhealthy behaviors, such as alcohol, drugs, self-harm, or eating problems. These behaviors are often used to try to hide painful emotions related to the abuse.

Under Title; 'IX of the Education Amendments of 1972', our school systems have a responsibility to deal with mental traumas in the following ways:

- Staff members need to be trained in how to deal with trauma-sensitive situations and know how to connect students with the right school-based mental health services, whether the events happen on or off school grounds. Any kind of stress can make it hard for a student to learn in school.
- Stress-sensitive schools may help all of their students do better, even those who have been through stress in the past. Policies and procedures that keep children safe should be used together with practices that are sensitive to trauma.
- Specialized instructional support staff, like school psychologists, counselors, nurses, and social workers, need to be involved because few programs that prepare future teachers include parts that help teachers learn the skills and coping strategies they need to spot and teach students who have been traumatized.
- There are many types of mental health help at school, such as on-site clinical services, positive behavior supports, social and emotional learning programs, efforts to get students involved, and building strong, supportive relationships with teachers.
- Schools can offer mental health services through their own clinical staff or by working with community mental health groups to accept requests when necessary. These services and supports may be used to deal with events, but trauma-informed practices and strong mental health supports will also help build social and emotional skills in students and make the school a better place to be.

The Long-term Consequences of Childhood Trauma

Sexual abuse of children is a grave problem that can have long-lasting effects on their physical and mental health, as well as on their general development and the relationships they will have in the future. A lot of studies have shown that this kind of abuse can have serious and long-lasting effects on a child's life.

Mental health is one of the most important effects of sexual abuse of children. It is more possible for people who have been sexually abused as children to have depression, anxiety, and post-traumatic stress disorder (PTSD). These conditions can show up in many ways, such as chronic sadness, hopelessness, fear, and anxiety. Victims may also have dreams, flashbacks, and unwanted thoughts that are related to the abuse, which can make it hard for them to function and enjoy life in general.

Child sexual abuse can also have a big effect on how a child develops sexually and how they get along with others. Teenagers who have been sexually abused may do dangerous things like sexual acts without thinking, using drugs, and hurting themselves. They might also pull away from people and settings that remind them of the abuse. This can make people feel alone, which can make their sadness and anxiety worse.

The long-term effects of child sexual abuse can also depend on how bad the tragedy was and how many times it happened. PTSD, sadness, and anxiety are more likely to happen to kids who have been through a lot of bad things and didn't get much help from their parents. They may also have trouble trusting people, which makes it hard for them to build good relationships with adults.

It's important to remember, though, that not all kids who are sexually abused will have long-term problems. Many kids can get better and live healthy, happy lives with the help of an understanding adult and good treatment. This makes it clear how important it is for caregivers and mental health workers to help and step in when a child has been sexually abused.

Child sexual abuse is a very bad problem that can have long-lasting effects on a child's physical and mental health, as well as on their general development and the relationships they will have in the future. It is very important for kids who have been sexually abused to get the help and therapy they need to get better and avoid long-term effects. *"Abuse is like a boomerang,"* one child said in a very moving way. It can hurt you again if you don't deal with it. To make sure our children are safe and successful in the future, we must make stopping and treating child sexual abuse a top priority.

References

- The AACAP (American Academy of Child Adolescent & Psychiatry)
- NCTSN "National Child Traumatic Stress Network"
- CMHS-Center for Mental Health Services
- SAMHSA- Substance Abuse and Mental Health Services Administration
- U.S. Department of Health and Human Services
- UCLA and Duke University
- U.S. Department of Health and Human Services, Administration on Children Youth and Families. (2007). Child Maltreatment 2005. Washington, DC: U.S. Government Printing Office.
- London, K., Bruck, M., Ceci, S.J., & Shuman, D.W. (2005). Disclosure of child sexual abuse: What does the research tell us about the ways that children tell? Psychology, Public Policy, and Law, 11 (1), 194–226.
- Deblinger, E., Lippmann, J., Steer, R. (1996). Sexually abused children suffering posttraumatic stress symptoms: Initial treatment outcome findings. Child Maltreatment, 1 (4), 310-321.
- Cohen, J.A., Mannarino, A.P., Deblinger, E. (2006). Treating trauma and traumatic grief in children and adolescents. New York: Guilford Press.
- Deblinger, E., Stauffer, A.H. (1996). Treating sexually abused children and their non-offending parents: A cognitive behavioral approach. Thousand Oaks, CA: Sage.

- The Centre for Addiction and Mental Health (CAMH) is Canada's largest mental health teaching hospital and one of the world's leading research centers in its field. CAMH is fully affiliated with the University of Toronto and is a Pan American
- LEWIS + LLEWELLYN, LLP
- CDC.gov (Center for Disease Control and Prevention)
- U.S. Department of Education, Office for Civil Rights.
- Title IX of the Education Amendments of 1972 (Title IX)
- National Association of School Psychologists. (2015). Research summaries: Creating trauma sensitive schools: supportive policies and practices for learning.
- U.S. Department of Health and Human Services, Administration on Children, Youth, and Families.

Milton Keynes UK
Ingram Content Group UK Ltd.
UKHW020727121124
451038UK00018B/351